# No Longer Forgotten

# No Longer Forgotten

## The Triumphs and Struggles of Rural Education in America

Edited by Michael Q. McShane
and Andy Smarick

ROWMAN & LITTLEFIELD
*Lanham • Boulder • New York • London*

Published by Rowman & Littlefield
A wholly owned subsidiary of The Rowman & Littlefield Publishing Group, Inc.
4501 Forbes Boulevard, Suite 200, Lanham, Maryland 20706
www.rowman.com

Unit A, Whitacre Mews, 26–34 Stannary Street, London SE11 4AB

British Library Cataloguing in Publication Information Available

**Library of Congress Cataloging-in-Publication Data Available**

ISBN: 978-1-4758-4607-2 (cloth : alk. paper)
ISBN: 978-1-4758-4608-9 (pbk. : alk. paper)
ISBN: 978-1-4758-4609-6 (electronic)

∞™ The paper used in this publication meets the minimum requirements of American National Standard for Information Sciences—Permanence of Paper for Printed Library Materials, ANSI/NISO Z39.48–1992.

Printed in the United States of America

# Contents

# Acknowledgments

This volume would not have been possible without the diligent work of numerous individuals whose names will not appear in the table of contents.

Our contributors presented drafts of their chapters at a research conference held at the American Enterprise Institute (AEI) in December 2017. We would like to thank Lilian Lowery of the Education Trust, Emily Freitag of Instruction Partners, and Jillian Balow, superintendent of schools for the state of Wyoming, who served as discussants at that event and prodded authors to refine and improve their arguments. We'd also like to thank the wonderful conference staff at AEI whose professionalism made the event a rousing success.

We'd also like to thank the AEI education policy program staffers who helped with editing and formatting the chapters of this volume, principally Grant Addison, who managed the project, as well as Amy Cummings, Rebecca Marquis, and Matthew Rice.

As always, we would like to thank Arthur Brooks, the stalwart leader of the AEI; Ryan Streeter, director of domestic policy studies at AEI; and Rick Hess, director of the Education Policy Studies Department at AEI, all of whom were supportive throughout this project. We'd also like to thank Robert Enlow, president and CEO of EdChoice, for his support.

# Introduction

## Michael Q. McShane and Andy Smarick

According to the National Center on Education Statistics, in the 2013–2014 school year, 9,132,607 children attended 27,264 schools in 7,156 districts that statisticians classify as "rural." Given this huge number of children, schools, and districts, one would assume that scholars have produced mountains of research on rural schools and that those involved in education-policy conversations would know granular details about rural children and their schools. That assumption would be incorrect.

In reality, precious little scholarship exists on rural schools, often shunted to specialized journals that have not been able to integrate their findings into the broader education-policy conversation. Our ignorance about the workings of rural schools has several negative consequences.

First, and most obviously, it means that we (education researchers *and* citizens) don't know what is going on in the schools that educate close to 20 percent of all students in the United States. But, on a deeper level, the asymmetry of attention placed on urban schools versus rural schools exacerbates broader trends in our politics and society that pit urban and rural citizens against each other. To care about one type of school does not mean that one doesn't care about others.

This volume seeks to broaden and deepen our collective understanding of rural education in America. But, before it can do that, we need to take some time to frame some key issues. First, when we say "rural," what do we mean? As it turns out, there is a great deal of debate as to how to classify schools and the communities in which they are located.

Second, we have to provide some background about the milieu in which rural schools operate. Several chapters in this volume will go into much greater detail, but we would like to walk through the major trends to facilitate continuity and clarity throughout the rest of the volume.

Third, we would like to explain the philosophical orientation of this volume, emphasizing that we believe rural communities have strengths like social cohesion and hometown pride that can be built upon to improve schools. Finally, we want to introduce some key questions that the authors in this volume will wrestle with in the subsequent pages.

## DEFINING RURAL

The term "rural" evokes different imagery for different people. For those in the Northeast, it can mean dense forests of evergreen trees, snowshoeing in the winter, and hiking and camping in the summer. In the mountains of Appalachia, particularly with accounts like *Hillbilly Elegy* dominating the popular consciousness, rugged, rural beauty and the Scots-Irish people who migrated there are juxtaposed with crushing problems of addiction, family decline, and economic devastation.

Across the South, the cotton fields once picked by slaves still produce fluffy white balls of fiber every fall after sweating through the steamy, humid summertime. As we head West across the great plains, the amber waves of grain of the Midwest become deserts in the South and mountains in the North, with vast expanses dotted with little frequency by small farming or mining communities. By the time we hit the Pacific Ocean, we have seen huge topographic, demographic, cultural, economic, and political difference in places all lumped into "Rural America."

How can we talk in an accurate, nuanced way about such an expansive, diverse category? For that, we frequently call on statisticians, who are adept at segmenting and analyzing such things. But even for our bean-counting friends, defining rurality is a challenge. The U.S. Census Bureau views it thus as follows: "The U.S. Census Bureau defines rural as what is not urban—that is, after defining individual urban areas, rural is what is left."[1] Other agencies view it differently. In fact, according to a 2016 speech by Dr. Alan Morgan, CEO of the National Rural Health Association, the federal government uses seventy-two different definitions for "rural" across agencies and programs.[2]

Perhaps a better understanding of rurality is cultural. Rural communities share several common characteristics. They are often small and close-knit. Generally speaking, a significant portion of the community is in some way tied to the land—through farming, mining, drilling, or something similar. And, they are typically isolated. Major cultural and civic institutions are more frequently found in cities and suburban areas with more population density— meaning rural families need to travel some distance to take advantage of large hospitals, professional sports stadiums, shopping malls, and the like.

That said, there is enormous variability within and between rural communities. As Nat Malkus will demonstrate in chapter 1, the rurality of the far West is different from the rurality of the Northeast or South. As he points out, while nationally 28 percent of rural students are nonwhite, in the South it is 36 percent, and in West it is 45 percent. In the West, 30 percent of rural students are Hispanic; only 5 percent are in the Midwest and Northeast. In the Northeast, only 10 percent of rural students live in poverty; in the South it is 21 percent, in the Midwest it is 13 percent, and in the West it is 17 percent.

We must also remember that there are stories from rural communities that are told with less frequency. As Sheneka Williams details in chapter 2, there is a substantial African-American rural population that stretches across a swathe from the "Black Belt" (named after the rich black soil of the region) of central Mississippi and Alabama through Georgia, before turning north through the Carolinas and ending in southern Virginia. If one overlays a map of the current African-American population with historical location of slave plantations, one still sees a great deal of overlap. This is a story seldom told when we speak of "rural" communities.

All of this is to say that there is no one satisfying definition of "rurality," either statistically, geographically, or historically. Defining it simply by what it is not seems inappropriate; but, to be honest, we don't have a better way of demarking the boundaries. To cope with this in a volume where authors from various disciplines will tackle issues across the spectrum of human experiences, we have decided to have authors use the definitions of the statistical agencies charged with collecting data for their particular issue area (health policy, economic, education, etc.).

We've asked them to be clear about which definitions they are using so that readers understand what they mean when they speak of "rural," even if the overlap between chapters isn't perfect. It is, admittedly, an imperfect solution, but it allows our authors to stay faithful to their disciplines' approaches, and it serves as a reminder of one of the fundamental challenges of studying rural schools.

## THE MILIEU

Now that that is out of the way, we can help set the stage for the conversation to follow. While there is diversity within rural communities, there are some common issues that we must place in the foreground before we can get to education.

Nonurban communities have been buffeted by several macroeconomic trends over the past several decades, as Angela Rachidi will detail in chapter 5. While most contemporary metropolitan areas are dominated by service industries, rural communities tend toward goods-producing industries like agriculture or manufacturing. As our economy transitions away goods production, rural communities are hit harder. More isolated areas have fewer options to replace lost jobs when a plant closes or a crop's value drops. This starts a vicious cycle of unemployment that is difficult to rectify.

Coupled with that, as Clayton Hale and Sally Satel detail in chapter 3, rural communities—particularly, but not exclusively, in Appalachia—have also been decimated by the opioid crisis. Opioids, powerful painkillers that tens of thousands of Americans are currently addicted to, are killing people in rural communities at staggering rates. Clayton and Sally put hard numbers on this crisis, like the more than 33,000 people who died from opioid overdoses in 2015 (more than those killed by car crashes, and twice as many as were killed by gun homicides) and the 2.7 million grandparents who are raising their grandchildren because the children's parents are addicted.

Education plays a role in both trying to break the cycle of unemployment. As Nat Malkus describes in chapter 1, rural communities have the highest percentage of idle adults between the age of eighteen and twenty-four (adults who are neither working nor in school) in the nation. While in urban areas, idleness has remained steady at 10 percent of the eighteen- to twenty-four-year-old population, rural communities have seen an increase in recent years. It now sits at 15 percent. This is one place where education comes in: In 2016, 45 percent of rural high school dropouts were idle.

In light of all of this, rural schools are asked to do a lot. They are seen as the front lines fighting against unemployment, idleness, and drug abuse. They are also the heart of many communities, unifying sparsely populated areas around Friday night football, homecoming parades, cheerleading competitions, plays, concerts, and dances.

Rural schools are often asked to do this, as Sara Dahill-Brown and Ashley Jochim point out in chapter 4, in isolation. While urban and suburban communities have dense networks of social service agencies and deep well of social capital, rural schools are often on their own to be a one-stop shop for the needs of the young people of their communities.

As Dahill-Brown and Jochim also point out, rural schools are also affected by broader American trends in political polarization that pit rural and urban communities against each other. Rural communities are more skeptical of state and federal intervention, believing that "outsiders" are ignorant or disrespectful of their value and values. In a 2017 survey, while 49 percent of urban respondents agreed that people in rural communities "shared their values," only 29 percent of rural respondents did.[3]

In more survey data Dahill-Brown and Jochim cite, rural respondents are more likely to blame government for recent hardships and more likely to believe that government helps big cities more than them. Insofar as education is a government enterprise managed by policies set at the state and federal levels, this is a recipe for problems.

Economics, health, and politics are all headwinds to rural schools as they try to meet the needs of the millions of children who walk in their doors.

## MOVING BEYOND A DEFICIT MIND-SET

Unfortunately, too many analyses of rural education stop after describing the problems outlined earlier. Doing so does a great disservice to rural communities. It also stunts analyses of rural education and precludes the development of workable solutions. Any serious study of rural education must move beyond a deficit mind-set and focus on building on the strengths of rural communities and the citizens who inhabit them.

First, we should start by stating that academic performance in rural areas offers much to celebrate. As Nat Mallkus details in chapter 1, while rural communities trail their suburban peers in terms of student achievement, they tend to outperform urban areas. Rural children, on average, arrive at school more ready to learn than their urban peers, and graduate from high school at higher rates as well. Are all of these schools as strong as they could be? No. Are they completely lost in trying to educate children? No, not at all. There is a strong foundation that better policies and practice can build on.

Second, as Dahill-Brown and Jochim demonstrate in chapter 4, rural communities enjoy more cohesion than urban communities. In a survey they cite, while only 57 percent of respondents living in cities believe that their neighbors shared their values, 74 percent of rural respondents did. Insofar as education is a social enterprise, and one in which elected school boards have to make decisions for an entire community, social cohesion can be a great asset. Having a shared vision and shared expectations can unite schools and ease the tensions and frictions that exist in schools that serve less cohesive populations.

Third, rural communities can be imbued with an unusual level of pride—in their history, culture, traditions, work, and more. When trying to improve schools, this is a great asset. Given that most school accountability systems in some way involve making performance known publicly, schools in proud communities can leverage that pride to make their schools better: *We don't want to look bad when the school scores get published, so let's get to work.*

This is not to say that there are not tensions at play when we talk about improving rural education.

The first is a big one: *What is the purpose of rural education today and in the near future?* Opinions differ. Many place workforce preparation at the top of the list. Many rural economies are atrophying while idleness and drug abuse are skyrocketing, so schools, it's argued, should be preparing young people for the workforce.

For some, this means getting students into four-year universities where they can be prepared for a wide range of potential occupations and make connections that might only exist outside of the small community that they came from. For others, this means getting students into high-quality career-and-technical-education programs in high school or at a community college near to their home. Local industries can work with schools to design curriculum that meets their needs: kids get jobs; everyone wins.

Still others see a very different primary goal of rural education. Many people live in rural areas for cultural, not economic, reasons. For them, education is about imparting the values and traditions of their community on their children. They see schools as bulwarks against a homogenizing of culture and an attack on the values of self-determination and traditional morality that they hold dear. Preparing students for the workforce is all well and good, but if that causes them to leave behind the values and culture of their families and communities, it is too high of a price to pay.

There can be conflict here between what might be best for individual students and what might be best for the community. On an individual level, the "brain drain" suffered by rural communities might be great. Young people from rural communities could be leaving for outstanding job options in cities where they will go on to lead happy, fulfilling, and productive lives.

As noted in Dahill-Brown and Jochim's chapter, research finds that for some rural areas, students' best path to upward economic mobility is to leave their communities behind. Unfortunately, that bright, happy, productive young person's departure leaves a bright, happy, productive young-person-sized hole in the community. It would be much better for the community if she stayed. Whose interests should take priority? It is not clear.

This first tension leads to a second: *If rural communities are dying, shouldn't schools help students get out?* Sheneka Williams quotes a graduate of a rural school in chapter 2 as saying he was "moving forward to give back." This crystalizes the tension perfectly.

Are rural schools preparing students who will leave for bigger and better opportunities outside of that community because there will be no jobs there in five to ten years? Are they preparing students who will return to reinvigorate their communities, to prevent those communities from dying? Is there some happy medium whereby graduates of rural schools can keep one foot in both worlds? Again, the answer is not clear.

It's also not clear what the future holds for rural communities. Rural communities do have many assets that could be valuable in the future. As the cost of living of major metropolitan areas rises, the ability of individuals to work remotely increases, and innovations like self-driving cars and virtual reality might make transportation and communication across great distances much quicker and better; perhaps, rural communities have a bright future after a rough few years. We simply don't know. Saying today that getting kids out is the best thing for them might turn out to be incredibly short-sighted.

One thing is clear, however; to date, many conversations about improving rural education have centered on one idea: online education. Now, we're not here to weigh the relative merits of online education or to talk about how it could be used to ameliorate the issues faced by rural schools. Juliet Squire will touch on online education briefly in chapter 8; and frankly, there are reams of writing about online education out there if it is of interest to you.

Helpful though it may be, many, if not most, of the issues raised in this volume *would not* be solved by online education. Online education might be *part* of a solution, but it is neither necessary nor sufficient to solve the problems in the subsequent pages of this volume. We have, quite deliberately, not devoted a chapter to online education and did not push authors to talk about online education where they did not feel that it was necessary.

## THE VOLUME AHEAD

One edited volume on rural schools will not possibly adjudicate all of these conflicting issues. We want to be clear: this volume is not meant to be the end of the conversation on rural education. In fact, it is just the opposite. We hope that this volume will encourage observers to take greater interest in rural schools, fill many of the gaps in knowledge that we have about rural education, and better understand the ways in which popular education-policy conversations intersect with rural schools and the communities in which they are located.

That said, one edited volume on rural schools *can* bring into clarity some of the macro-issues facing rural schools. Nat Malkus provides an in-depth statistical analysis of rural school demographics and performance in chapter 1. In chapter 2, Sheneka Williams details both the history and personal experiences of African-American rural education and the myriad ways in which racism played a role in shaping rural schools in the American South. Clayton Hale and Sally Satel, in chapter 3, dive deeply into the opioid epidemic and its horrific consequences for young people and the schools that they attend.

An edited volume can also offer some hard data on and new thinking about the condition of rural schools and the politics that shape them. In chapter 4, Sara Dahill-Brown and Ashley Jochim provide what may be the research literature's first in-depth examination of the politics of rural education and the collection of contradictions that shape local school boards, the actions of superintendents, and state and federal policy on rural education. Angela

Rachidi, in chapter 5, looks at the economic trends affecting rural schools and the communities in which they are situated and will discuss what social welfare programs can do to help mitigate those issues.

A single volume can also discuss policy issues that affect rural schools. As James Shuls discusses in chapter 6, how do we pay for rural schools, and how do the peculiar ways we tax property make it so difficult to do so? As Daniel Player and Aliza Husain discuss in chapter 7, where do rural schools get their teachers, and how can they ensure a ready supply of quality educators into their buildings? As Juliet Squire examines in chapter 8, is there a role that charter schools can play?

Again, this volume aims to help catalyze a vigorous conversation about rural education in America. In a time of incredible polarization and tribalism, we hope to present a shared set of facts and data about how rural schools operate, how they are performing, and which big issues are affecting them. We also hope to offer some potential solutions.

From changing the way we recruit teachers to changing how we tax property to how we deploy chartering and autonomy in schools and districts, there are steps that can be taken to address some of these challenges. The list of potential solutions is not exhaustive, and some who agree with authors' descriptions of the problems at hand might quarrel with the solutions offered. This should not cause strife—in fact, quite the opposite. Our schools are perhaps the most important institutions in our nation, and passionate debate about them will only make them stronger.

## NOTES

1   Michael Ratcliffe, Charlynn Burd, Kelly Holder, and Alison Fields, "Defining Rural at the U.S. Census Bureau: American Community Survey and Geography Brief," U.S. Census Bureau, last modified December 2016, https://www2.census. gov/geo/pdfs/reference/ua/Defining_Rural.pdf.

2   Alan Morgan, "The Opioid Epidemic: The Rural Perspective," Housing Assistance Council, YouTube, December 9, 2016, https://www.youtube.com/watch? v=TlSp631NQcc&feature=youtu.be&t=3m30s.

3   Jose A. DelReal and Scott Clement, "Poll of Rural Americans Shows Deep Cultural Divide with Urban Centers," *Washington Post*, June 17, 2017, https://www. washingtonpost.com/amphtml/classic-apps/new-poll-of-rural-americans-shows-deep-cultural-divide-with-urban-centers/2017/06/16/d166c31e-4189–11e7–9869-bac8b446820a_story.html.

*Chapter 1*

# A Statistical Portrait of Rural Education in America

## Nat Malkus

What does "rural" mean? And how does rural life differ from life in cities, suburbs, or even small towns? Those can be difficult questions to answer. Ruralness isn't an aspect that many people find easy to describe, even if they know it when they see it. At a minimum, rural areas are defined by a low population density and an economy grounded—at least to some extent—in living off the land, through industries such as farming, mining, or timber.

Beyond these basic soft borders, the American idea of ruralness takes different forms in different contexts. For instance, for those hailing from the West, "rural" might reasonably evoke a picture of sparse desert expanses or mountain frontiers. In contrast, residents of the Midwest would sooner envision rural areas as more distinctly agrarian, with expansive farmland filling open spaces.

Still different, for those in the Northeast, "rural" may conjure bucolic rolling hills marked by occasional hamlets. In the South, "rural" may bring to mind the Mississippi Delta or Appalachian hill country. Of course, pictures of what "rural" is vary with context, but in each context they stand in stark contrast to urban areas. Whatever a rural area is, it is not a city.

When it comes to rural education, a similar question arises: What does rural education look like? And how does it differ from education in more urbanized areas? The antiquated notion of the one-room schoolhouse is a bygone fixture of an earlier era, but it was a recognizable form—whereas any current notions of rural schools and rural education are fairly amorphous.

Some of the same factors that apply to rural areas generally also mark differences for rural schools. Because they're located in sparsely populated areas, rural schools tend to be smaller than their more urban counterparts and thus struggle to offer as many specialized programs and services. Also, as rural graduates exit high school, their options may have looser links to the urban-centered economies than their urban peers have.

Beyond these scant basics, there are few specific differentiators for rural schools; their primary distinction is their general contrast from urban schools, which have garnered a disproportionate amount of attention from policymakers, education researchers, and popular media.

This chapter is an effort to sharpen the image of rural education. It draws on a variety of nationally representative data sources to paint a statistical portrait of America's rural schools. On the one hand, this portrait examines common factors that differentiate rural schools from their more urban counterparts. At the same time, it keeps an eye on where and how rural schools are heterogeneous, displaying more than one tendency. Overall, this portrait displays that rural schools enjoy some promising advantages, face particular challenges, and vary considerably from one region to another.

This statistical portrait is presented in four sections. Because it naturally relies on statistics, the "Defining Rural Areas for Statistical Purposes" section describes how schools are objectively categorized as rural, urban, and in-between. The "Rural Children's Experiences before Entering School" section overviews early childhood educational offerings in rural areas, including participation in day care, preschool, prekindergarten, and Head Start. It also looks at the proportion of rural students staying at home, attending center-based care, and variations in family structure.

The "Rural School Students and Operations" section examines rural schools, primarily focusing on public schools. It looks at how many students and schools are located in rural areas, the demographics of those students, and the programmatic offerings of their elementary and secondary schools. The "Rural Children's Experiences before Entering School" section examines the outputs and outcomes of students in rural schools. Outputs encompass the *results* of schooling, such as test scores and graduation rates, and the gaps in these outputs. Outcomes deal with the *steps* rural students take after school, including college-going and workforce entry.

Some elements of this portrait will not surprise you. Before school, young children of rural families are more likely to have stay-at-home parents. Rural students attend smaller schools with limited extracurricular programs. Rural schools also have relatively few poor and minority students, and their students have above-average test scores and graduation rates.

Other elements of this portrait, however, might surprise you. While young rural children have more stay-at-home parents, by the time they are three and four, their early childcare experiences are similar to their urban peers. Rural schools vary substantially across regions, with poor and minority students in the Northeast and Midwest constituting a fraction of the population in the

South and West. And while rural students have strong school outcomes on average, they face some limited opportunities after high school.

Before touring the varied landscape of rural education, however, we need a definition of what we mean by rural.

## DEFINING RURAL AREAS FOR STATISTICAL PURPOSES

The vagaries around the rural concept must yield to an objective form in order to have consistent measurement. Since this chapter draws primarily on data from the National Center for Education Statistics (NCES), its definition of rural is consistent and convenient.[1] Since 2006, NCES has used the same "urban-centric" locale definitions used by the U.S. Census Bureau. Fittingly, under this urban-centric definition, rural areas include all those located *outside* of places the Census calls "urban."

The urban umbrella term includes three locales: cities, suburbs, and towns. Each of these is broken into three subtypes: large, midsize, and small. City locales include territories within an urbanized area (which the U.S. Census Bureau defines as an area of 50,000 or more people)[2] and inside a principal city (the largest city in an urbanized area).[3] The city locale is further divided into large, midsize, and small sublevels according to their total populations—more than 250,000, between 100,000 and 250,000, and fewer than 100,000, respectively.

Suburban locales are territories within urbanized areas but outside of principal cities and are broken into sublevels by the same population levels as cities. Towns are areas located outside urbanized areas, but inside urban clusters (which the U.S. Census Bureau defines as areas with between 2,500 and 50,000 people), and are subcategorized by their distance from an urbanized area.

Anything outside of these three urban locales is considered rural. Rural areas are categorized as either "fringe," "distant," or "remote" according to their distances from urbanized areas or clusters. Rural fringe areas are nearest to urban locales—less than or equal to 5 miles from urbanized area or less than or equal to 2.5 miles from an urban cluster. Distant rural areas are more than 5, but less than 25 miles from an urbanized area, or 2,5 to 10 miles from an urban cluster. Remote rural areas are the furthest from urbanized areas, by more than twenty-five miles, or further than ten miles from an urban cluster.

While there are important differences between the rural subcategories, the essence of rural-ness in this classification is the distinction from urban places—or, in Census parlance, urbanized areas and clusters—and those essential distinctions tend to only grow with distance. For this reason, this chapter uses the entire rural locale instead of rural sublevels.

One wrinkle in NCES's classification system is that while every *school* can be specifically accounted for as belonging to one locale, school *districts* can include schools from different locale classifications. For example, a district classified as "suburban" might include a number of individual schools that are classified as "rural." Despite the partial mismatch between the locale of some schools and the districts they belong to, there are valuable reasons to compare school districts by their predominant locale.

For instance, districts, rather than schools, are the ones that often deal with issues like transportation or providing opportunities for advanced course-taking, which pose unique challenges in rural areas. In order to compare districts by locale, the chapter uses NCES district categorizations, which assign a locale based on the predominant locale of the district's schools.

Of course, this classification system groups together a large number of schools into each locale category that are far from homogeneous. To illustrate differences between locales and across rural areas, select data points are broken out by locale to first illustrate rural differences, and then across regions to display the variation between one rural area and another. Any classification system is bound to group schools that are heterogeneous, and examining differences across regions is an effort to keep that rural diversity from being glossed over.

## RURAL CHILDREN'S EXPERIENCES BEFORE ENTERING SCHOOL

Reams of research have detailed how important family structure and early childhood experiences are to students' readiness for school and to their future educational outcomes. As such, it makes sense to begin with a portrait of rural education by looking at each of these factors for rural students.

### Rural Family Structure

According to 2012 data from the NCES Early Childhood Program Participation (ECPP) survey, 79 percent of rural families had two parents at home, slightly more than suburban families (74 percent) and markedly more than families living in towns or cities (70 and 63 percent, respectively).[4] The rural South breaks from the other regions with significantly fewer two-parent households than rural families in other regions (73 percent versus between 81 and 85 percent).

The ECPP data also provide some indications that young children in rural areas receive additional early educational supports at home. For instance, at 22 percent, the proportion of rural zero- to three-year-olds who were read to by a family member three or fewer times a week was lower than their peers in other locales. Half of these young rural children were read to an average of once a day, which was well above those in cities or towns. In sum, young children in rural environments have a number of home-based advantages heading into school, compared to those in other locales.

## Rural Early Childcare Arrangements

Given the dispersed population, it can seem logical that rural students' childcare experiences prior to entering kindergarten would differ from those in more population-dense, urban areas. However, rural patterns of childcare arrangements are quite similar to those in more urban locales.

According to the ECPP, about 46 percent of rural children aged zero to three stay at home with their parents without weekly alternative childcare arrangements. Roughly 25 percent had weekly center-based care arrangements, including day cares or preschools. About the same percentage have weekly care arrangements with relatives, and 16 percent have weekly arrangements with caregivers not related to them, such as a babysitter or nanny. (Some children have more than one type of arrangement, so these figures do not sum to 100 percent.)

Perhaps surprisingly, children aged zero to three in urban and suburban environments have a nearly identical breakdown. Children in towns have a slightly higher percentage that stay at home (51 percent) and a slightly lower percentage (18 percent) have weekly center-based care arrangements.

For children aged zero to five, the kinds of center-based care families used did not differ substantially between rural and more urban environments. The main difference in center-based care was the percentage in Head Start, a federal program for promoting low-income students' school-readiness. Twenty percent of rural zero- to five-year-olds attended Head Start at some point, which was well below the percentage in cities (30 percent) but above the percentage in both suburbs and towns.

A somewhat different pattern emerges for older children who are not yet attending kindergarten. Roughly a quarter of rural four- and five-year-olds stay at home, which is more than the percentages in cities, suburbs, and towns. In 2012, about 65 percent of rural four- and five-year-olds had weekly center-based care arrangements, which was similar to their urban peers, but lower than the percentage in either suburbs or towns.

Despite these minor differences, and the childcare challenges that might be assumed in rural areas with little population density, overall, the pattern of early childcare arrangements in rural areas is quite similar to those in more-urban locales. The distinctions between rural and more-urban students once they enter school do not appear to stem from the kinds of childcare arrangements available to rural families.

## Students at Kindergarten Entry

Children's readiness for school first comes into focus when they become students, and for most, that happens as they enter kindergarten. Differences in students' academic readiness are important at this point because, unfortunately, gaps that appear early on are often durable.

At entry, the math and reading skills of kindergartners in rural areas, as measured by the Early Childhood Longitudinal Study of 2011 (ECLS-K),[5] were not measurably different from those in suburban kindergartens. Both rural and suburban kindergartners scored above their peers in town kindergartens. Those differences were not statistically significant but are worth noting as they widen in later years to become larger and significant. Suburban and rural scores were also higher than those of kindergartners in cities. These differences, however, were large *and* significant—between 11 and 18 percent of a standard deviation (SD) in reading and math. These differences presage the gaps between locales that are evident in higher grades.

Across regions, rural kindergartners' math scores suggested variation that, while seldom statistically significant, also mirrors patterns that become larger and significant in later grades. Math scores of rural kindergartners in the South were lower than their peers in the Midwest and Northeast. Kindergartners in the West had relatively low scores in math, but they only differed measurably from kindergartners in the Northeast.

Most of these differences are relatively small and more meaningful for kindergartners in cities than those in other locales. However, they are important to gauge for rural children because these differences "at the starting gate" of schooling tend to grow in upper grades.

# RURAL SCHOOL STUDENTS AND OPERATIONS

There are many facets to include in a description of rural schools, and no particular order to place them in. This chapter first looks at who attends rural schools—that is, their demographics—and then what rural schools look like in terms of size, operations, and program offerings.

## Rural Student Race and Ethnicity

Rural schools educate a much higher percentage of white students—and lower percentages of minority students—than schools in towns, suburbs, or cities. In 2014–2015, 72 percent of students attending rural schools were non-Hispanic white, far above town and suburban schools (64 and 51 percent, respectively), and double the percentage for urban schools (29 percent).[6]

Hispanic students were the second-largest ethnic group across all locales, making up 13 percent of rural students. Just 19 percent of town schools' populations were Hispanic, accounting for almost all of the difference in nonwhite students between town and rural schools. Hispanic students made up twice the percentage in suburban than in rural schools, and urban schools had nearly three times the percentage of Hispanic students than rural schools (25 and 36 percent, respectively, versus 13 percent for rural schools).

Rural and town schools had 9 and 10 percent black students, respectively, while suburban and urban schools had larger shares (14 and 24 percent, respectively). Rural and town schools also had markedly lower percentages of Asian students, at 1 percent each, than urban and suburban schools (about 6 percent). Roughly 5 percent of students across all locales were from other racial categories.

Rural schools had the highest percentages of white and the lowest percentages of minority students across *locales*, but these demographics differ dramatically for rural areas across *regions*. Nationally, 28 percent of rural students were nonwhite, but the Northeast and Midwest had far smaller proportions of minority students, at just 12 percent. In comparison, schools in the rural South had three times that proportion, at 36 percent, and in the West, the multiple approached four, at 45 percent.

Black students constituted the highest proportion of nonwhite rural students in the South, at 16 percent, far above the overall rural average of 9 percent. More pointedly, the next highest regional rural black percentage was just 3 percent. Hispanic percentages also varied substantially, making up about 30 percent of rural students in the West, which is double the percentage in the South (14 percent), and six times the proportion in the rural Northeast or Midwest (about 5 percent).

In relative terms, rural schools are disproportionately white compared to more urban schools, both overall and within regions. However, in an absolute sense, rural schools are far more diverse in some regions than others.

## School Socioeconomic Status

Students in rural districts also display substantial differences in socioeconomic status, both compared to those in more urban districts and to other rural districts across regions. The Stanford Education Data Archive (SEDA), which includes publicly available data on all districts in the country, demonstrates variation in multiple aspects of socioeconomic status, which is strongly related to school resources and outcomes.[7]

Using a standardized, cumulative measure of socioeconomic status (with a mean of zero and an SD of one), students in urban districts were far poorer than other locales (33 percent of an SD below average), while those in town districts were moderately poorer (20 percent of an SD below average). Perhaps unsurprisingly, suburban districts stand in stark contrast to urban schools, with a much higher socioeconomic status (over half of an SD *above* average). Perhaps more surprising, rural districts were just above average overall, but well above both urban and town districts (by less than a tenth of an SD).

However, regional differences in rural district socioeconomic status were also stark. In the Northeast, the urban–rural divide is the largest, with urban districts two-thirds of an SD below average and rural districts a full half of an SD above—in total, well over an SD apart. The Midwest shows a similar pattern but has an urban–rural gap almost half the size (two-thirds of an SD). In contrast, urban–rural gaps in the South and West are considerably narrower.

Poverty rates—the proportion of the population that is below the federal poverty line—reflect similar patterns.[8] On average, urban districts have a poverty rate of 20 percent, and urban districts in all four regions are within three points of that average. Among rural districts, the average is 15 percent, but this varies considerably more across regions.

For example, rural districts in the Northeast have a 10 percent poverty rate, which is lower than any other locale, including suburbs. In the South, the rural poverty rate is just slightly above that of urban districts (21 versus 20 percent) but twice the rural poverty rate in the Northeast. Poverty rates in the Midwest and West lie at 13 and 17 percent, respectively.

Free-lunch data—the most common metric for poverty directly tied to schools—also mirror these patterns.[9] Similar to the socioeconomic status data discussed earlier, within regions, the Northeast and Midwest showed the widest urban–rural divides for free and reduced-cost meal rates, while gaps in the South and West were narrower. Looking *across* regions at rural schools, the differences are even more apparent. Less than one-third of rural students in the Northeast receive free lunch, compared to more than half of rural students in the South.

Across each of these socioeconomic measures, it is clear that rural schools and districts are advantaged relative to their town, and especially their urban, counterparts. Again, despite that relative advantage, rural schools are far from uniform socioeconomically, with the West and, particularly, the South, faring worse than the Midwest and Northeast.

## Students with Disabilities and English Language Learners

Two other student characteristics are particularly important in K–12 schooling: students with disabilities and students who are English language learners (ELLs). Across the nation, according to data on all public schools from the 2013–2014 Civil Rights Data Collection, about 12 percent of students are designated with a disability under the Individuals with Disabilities Education Act (IDEA).[10] That percentage does not vary across locales.

However, there are slight regional differences in the percentages of special-education students. The Northeast and Midwest have slightly above-average percentages of special-education students, while the West and South have slightly lower percentages. That same pattern of regional variation applies to rural schools but appears to be an attribute of regions, not of rural schools.

Almost 10 percent of students across the nation are ELLs, according to Civil Rights Data Collection (CRDC) data. Rural schools report lower ELL percentages than other locales, at 4 percent, and those percentages rise in towns, suburbs, and urban areas (7, 10, and 15 percent, respectively). There is also regional variation in the overall percentage of ELL students across all locales, with markedly higher percentages in the West (17 percent), below-average percentages in the Northeast and Midwest (6 percent each), and near the national average in the South (9 percent).

Rural schools have the lowest percentages of ELL students across all regions, but the differences between regions are dramatic. Only 1 percent of rural students in the Northeast are ELL students, doubling to only 2 percent in the rural Midwest. That percentage more than doubles again to 5 percent of students in the rural South, and again to 12 percent in the rural West. Again, rural schools stand apart from their more-urban counterparts but maintain significant diversity with above-average rates of ELL students in the West and half the average rate or lower in other regions.

## Rural Family Involvement in Schools

Beyond demographics, rural students' families show differences from families in other locales in terms of their involvement in school and communal events, despite their relative lack of population density. In other words, rural families seem more involved at school and church than families in other locales, despite the longer average travel times involved in rural areas.

According to 2012 data from the Parent and Family Involvement (PFI) survey, rural families report higher rates of parent involvement at school for most events asked about—including PTA meetings, parent–teacher conferences, fundraisers, school-based committees, or class or school events—than families in other locales.[11] These measures of parental engagement at school suggest that, despite the presumably greater travel distances from schools that rural families face, their engagement does not suffer.

Other reported activities from the PFI data back this notion. On the one hand, rural families reported that percentages of their K–12 students who visited libraries, bookstores, museums, concerts, and other place-based activities were smaller than those residing in cities or suburbs across the board, and smaller than most reports from families in towns. These reports are consistent with the notion that population density works against place-based activities for rural families. However, the case is not the same for the school-based activities listed earlier, nor is it the case for attending churches or religious institutions or athletic and sporting events.

These signals are certainly distinct from demographics but layer on top of differences in rural family structure and frequency of reading to young children to suggest that rural families may provide some advantages in terms of involvement and social-capital building compared to those in more urban locales.

## School Size and Offerings

In 2014–2015—the most recent data available from NCES's Common Core of Data—more than 9.2 million students attended rural elementary and secondary schools across the United States.[12] They constituted 18 percent of the nation's students—far above the 11 percent in town schools, but far less than those attending city or suburban schools (30 and 40 percent, respectively).

Not surprising given dispersed rural populations, rural schools are smaller than their more-urban counterparts, making the proportion of rural schools, 28 percent, much higher than the proportion of students. On average, rural schools serve 344 students, which is smaller compared to those in towns, suburbs, or cities (432, 647, and 581 students, respectively).

Rural school districts are also smaller, containing relatively fewer schools and thus making up a larger share of districts. Over half of the nation's districts are predominantly rural, while urban districts—which educate a far larger number of students—make up only 6 percent. Predominately suburban and town districts make up 23 and 18 percent, respectively.

The smaller size of both rural schools and districts deprives them of some of the economies of scale that their suburban and urban counterparts enjoy. For instance, rural schools have fewer students per teacher, at roughly 14.5, than schools in cities, suburbs, or towns—which have just over 16 or 17 students per teacher. However, rural student-to-teacher ratios vary across regions. While rural schools in the Midwest and South are close to the average of 14.5, those in the Northeast have lower ratios at about 12.5 students per teacher. In the West, rural schools have higher ratios at seventeen students per teacher.

These differences are hard to map because they are composed at once of both rural effects (relatively low student-to-teacher ratios compared to other locales) and regional differences (lower ratios in the Northeast and higher in the West). The important points to remember are that, at the same time, rural areas can differ systematically from more urban ones, and they can still vary substantially across regions.

Small class sizes can be beneficial, of course, but the pattern of resources suggests rural schools are facing constraints that lead to higher costs, rather than making intentional decisions. For instance, the number of pupils per administrative staff (including administrators and administrative support staff) in rural districts, at under 200, was far below that in town, suburban, and urban districts (which approached 300, 350, and 375 pupils per administrator, respectively).

Furthermore, rural schools have fewer specialized staff to serve particular student needs. According to the 2015–2016 National Teacher and Principal Survey,[13] the percentage of rural schools employing specialists and instructional coaches (55 percent) was smaller than town schools (60 percent), and substantially smaller than suburban and urban schools (71 and 73 percent, respectively).[14]

Specialized services are also less available in rural schools. About 55 percent of rural schools offered instruction beyond the normal school day for students who need academic assistance, compared to 68 percent in urban schools. Also, 37 percent of rural schools offered instruction for students seeking academic enrichment or advancement compared to 54 percent of city schools. Only 21 percent of rural and town schools offer day care for students who need it, while more than twice that percentage of city and suburban schools do so.

Not only are staff and services less specialized, but also fewer rural schools offer specializations. About 92 percent of rural schools are considered "regular schools," compared to 81 percent of urban schools and about 88 percent of suburban and town schools. About 8 percent of city schools and 3 percent of suburban schools offer special-emphasis programs—such as special education or career and technical schools—compared to around 1 percent of town and rural schools.

This lack of specialization available in rural schools can also be seen in student course-taking. For instance, 2,009 rural high school graduates earned an average of 2.85 credits in advanced courses, while their peers in urban schools earned 4.2 and those in suburban schools earned 4.6.

Rural schools have particular difficulty offering Advanced Placement (AP) courses and have lagged far behind other locales for years. In 2012, less than two-thirds of rural schools offered AP courses, compared to 77, 82, and 91 percent of town, urban, and suburban schools, respectively.[15] AP course credit-earning reflects these differences, where city and suburban students earned 74 and 94 percent more credits than rural students on average.

These same differences exist for foreign-language credits (26 and 29 percent higher in city and suburban schools, respectively, than rural schools), for honors courses (23 and 53 percent higher), and for calculus (30 and

37 percent). These extra resources give urban and suburban students a leg up in their efforts to get to college.

To compensate for the lack of on-site opportunities, rural schools often look to alternative offerings for their students. For instance in 2015–2016, 33 percent of rural schools offered courses entirely online—a higher proportion than town, city, and suburban schools (22, 17, and 16 percent, respectively).[16] Based on data from the High School Longitudinal Study, among 2,009 ninth graders who were enrolled in college in 2013, more than a third of students in city and suburban schools received college credit in high school, compared to only 26 percent of students in rural schools.[17]

However, a higher percentage of college students from rural high schools received college credit from dual-enrollment courses—28 percent, compared to 20 percent or less of students from city and suburban schools. As a result, the percentage of rural students who took no courses for college credit was not significantly different across city, suburban, and rural school graduates.

## SCHOOL OUTCOMES FOR RURAL STUDENTS

There are two ways to examine student outcomes across locales: by looking at individual students and by looking at school average scores. The best natural source for student data in reading and mathematics is the National Assessment of Educational Progress (NAEP).[18] NAEP provides data on students in fourth, eighth, and twelfth grades across the country, and gives representative measures for locales overall and, in some cases, by region. The other measurement of student outcomes, state-assessment scores, is collected in the ED*Facts* data available from the NCES and gives school-level scores for every school in the nation.[19] This section looks at both sets of data to examine student outcomes in rural schools.

### Rural Student Achievement

For both reading and math scores across fourth, eighth, and twelfth grades, rural students scored above urban students but below suburban students across the board. These differences were relatively small—roughly four points on NAEP or about a tenth of an SD above and below rural students.

However, these differences are not evident across all regions, primarily because rural students score quite differently from one region to the next. Figure 1.1 illustrates this point. From 2007 to 2015, suburban students scored higher than (or not measurably different from) rural students on NAEP eighth-grade reading, with students from towns scoring somewhat lower and students from urban locales scoring lowest of all. Across these years, rural students in the Northeast scored well above the national average for suburban students, and rural student scores in the Midwest were higher than, or no different from, the suburban average, as shown in Figure 1.2.

On the other hand, in the West and South, rural students had much lower scores. While none of these differences are statistically significant, the pattern

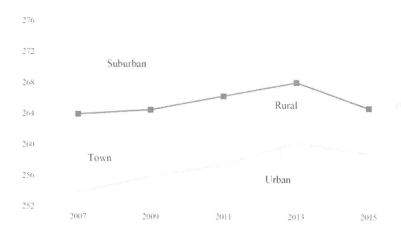

**Figure 1.1** **NAEP Eighth-Grade Reading Scores by Locale.** *Source:* **National Center for Education Statistics**

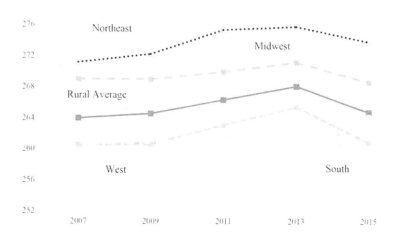

**Figure 1.2** **NAEP Eighth-Grade Rural Reading Scores by Region.** *Source:* **National Center for Education Statistics**

is clear: There is more regional variation *within* the rural student scores than there is *across* locales nationally. The range between locales in 2015 was about nine points, while rural student scores across regions differed by roughly thirteen points.

This variation in rural student scores means that the rural–urban divide isn't a constant; it's evident only in particular regions. For instance, the rural advantage over urban students in reading and math across all three grades—which, overall, is between five and six points on NAEP—is primarily driven by the gap in the Northeast (which, for all three grades, are three times this average) and by the Midwest (where gaps are roughly double this average).

In contrast, there is no rural–urban divide in the South, where scores are within one or two points, and the divide in the West is about equal to the average of five or six points. Suburban schools show a different pattern, where the predominant differences with rural students are found in the South, with smaller or no differences in the Northeast and Midwest. In the West, rural students' scores are either equivalent to or higher than suburban students' scores.

These scores are consistent with the smaller gaps evident in the section on school readiness at kindergarten entry, discussed earlier. They also reflect variation seen in other demographic characteristics, where rural schools display a consistent advantage relative to urban schools, but that within rural schools, important differences in absolute scores reveal how different rural schools are across the country.

## Rural Student Achievement Gaps

Of course, overall scores are not the only concern when it comes to student outcomes. Achievement gaps, or differences in scores between student groups, provide a view into how equitable outcomes are—and these, too, differ across locales. Figure 1.3 illustrates black-white (black double lines) and Hispanic-white (gray lines) grade four reading gaps across city, suburban, and rural schools over time. Both gaps are highest in cities, where average test scores differ by roughly thirty points or 83 percent of an SD.

In rural schools, the black-white score gaps are substantially smaller, between nineteen and twenty-four points—two-thirds the size of urban gaps. The difference is even greater for the Hispanic-white gap, which in rural schools in 2015 approached half the gap in urban schools. Suburban and town (not shown) gaps were in between. While none of these differences are statistically significant, they are consistent across reading and math scores; across grades four, eight, and twelve; and across all years from 2007 to 2015.

Test-score gaps by poverty, as measured by free and reduced-priced lunch, show similar patterns to those by race. Figure 1.4 maps these gaps in grade eight NAEP reading scores. Free and reduced-priced lunch gaps were largest

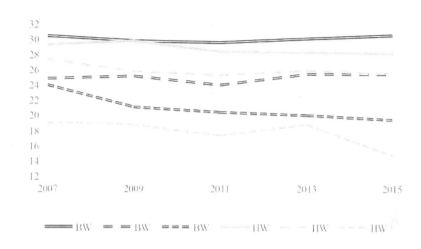

Figure 1.3   NAEP Fourth-Grade Black-White and Hispanic-White Reading Gaps by Locale, 2007 to 2015. *Source:* National Center for Education Statistics

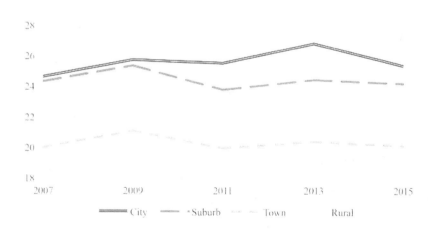

Figure 1.4   NAEP Eighth-Grade Free and Reduced-Price Lunch Reading Gaps by Locale, 2007 to 2015. *Source:* National Center for Education Statistics

in urban and suburban schools across all years, at roughly twenty-five points, or two-thirds of an SD. Town and rural poverty score gaps were smaller across all years, at about twenty points on the NAEP scale—just over half of an SD.

Overall, these student outcomes show that rural students perform relatively well in school, especially compared to urban and town students. These advantages are not directly attributable to the schools being rural, however, as rural schools have fewer poor and minority students, who on average tend to perform more poorly on assessments than higher-income and white students. However, there may be more to rural schools than just the sum of their demographic differences, as the gaps by race and poverty are systematically smaller in rural schools than in more urban areas.

## Rural Graduation Rates

While suburban students and schools tend to edge out their rural counterparts in terms of academic scores, rural graduates have the highest overall graduation rates of all locales. According to 2014–2015 ED*Facts* graduation rate data, urban schools had the lowest rate at 79.5 percent.[20] In addition, urban schools also showed the greatest variation in graduation rates, with the difference between the 25th and 75th percentiles (also known as the interquartile range) of urban-school graduation rates 18 percentile points apart.

Town and suburban schools had higher graduation rates at 86 and 87 percent, respectively, and comparably smaller interquartile ranges of between ten and twelve points. Rural schools boast the highest graduation rate at nearly 89 percent and had the smallest interquartile range, at less than 10 percentage points.

Rural graduation rates showed less variation across regions than other characteristics in this chapter. In each region except the West, rural schools had the highest graduation rate across locales, and in the West only suburban rates were higher. In the Northeast and Midwest, rural graduation rates were 91 percent, 15 full percentage points above their urban rates. Rural graduation rates were near the rural average in the South, at 88 percent, and lower in the West at 84 percent. In both the West and the South, the rural–urban graduation-rate divide was far smaller than in the Northeast and Midwest, between 3 and 6 percentage points.

## Rural Opportunities after School

While graduation rates in rural schools are relatively encouraging, college-going rates for these graduates are less so. According to High School Longitudinal Study data from 2013, 71 percent of rural students went to some form of college, which was less than 76 percent of urban and 79 percent of suburban students who did so.[21] Again, there was regional variation here, with rural students in the West and South going to college at lower rates (69 percent) than rural students from the Northeast and Midwest (75 and 76 percent, respectively).

In addition, rural students are less likely than their more urban counterparts to go to a four-year college. Compared to an average of 32 percent of all students, about 29 percent of rural students were seeking a bachelor's degree a year after graduation. In the West, only 18 percent of rural graduates did so.

These differences in college attendance are not entirely unexpected, at least from parent perspectives. Looking again at the PFI survey, lower percentages of parents of sixth- through twelfth-grade students in rural areas expected their children to earn a graduate degree or a bachelor's degree than parents in urban or suburban locales.

In contrast, higher percentages of rural parents expected their students would graduate only from high school or attend a vocational or technical school. Parents living in towns had similar or lower educational expectations for their students. While not all these data are statistically significant, the pattern is consistent both with lower expectations for educational attainment among rural families and their lower rates of college-going.

These may seem like small differences in college-going and the pursuit of bachelor's degrees. However, these differences are all the more important for rural students because the prospects for those students without further education are direr in rural areas. According to America Community Survey data, the share of adults aged eighteen to twenty-four who are idle—that is, neither in work nor attending school—is higher in rural areas than in other locales, and this rural idleness is getting worse over time.[22]

Between 2006 and 2016, about 10.5 percent of all American eighteen- to twenty-four-year-olds were idle. The percentage of idle adults in urban areas was roughly the same in both years, at about 10 percent. In contrast, 12 percent of rural eighteen- to twenty-four-year-olds were idle in 2006, which grew to 15 percent ten years later. In both years, female eighteen- to twenty-four-year-olds had higher rates of idleness than males, and this was decidedly more pronounced in rural areas.

The growth in idleness was also more pronounced for certain groups. In 2006, about 8 percent of rural eighteen- to twenty-four-year-old males were idle, which increased by half to over 12 percent ten years later. However, the growth in rural idleness is primarily driven by white eighteen- to twenty-four-year-olds, as percentages of idle non-Hispanic black and Hispanic rural adults this age actually dropped.

Of course, white adults make up a much larger share of the overall rural population compared to other localities, which is reflected in the relatively lower minority populations in rural schools noted earlier. The percentage of eighteen- to twenty-four-year-olds who were idle was also markedly higher for those living below the poverty line, at 29 percent, and for those living in the South and West, at 16 and 22 percent, respectively. The most dramatic difference, however, was evident for rural high school dropouts, 45 percent of whom were idle, up 13 percentage points over just ten years.

## CONCLUSION

This statistical portrait combines a wide array of data to depict how rural education differs from education in other locales. However, it may be unsatisfying for those looking for a simple description. Overall, three points are worth considering in summary.

First, while there are clear, relative differences between rural education and that in other locales in terms of inputs and outcomes, there remain considerable absolute differences *within* rural areas. Second, some of the challenges of providing education for rural students lead to different kinds of operations and offerings. Finally, for all the challenges rural education faces, rural students enjoy a number of advantages, and perhaps less inequality, than do their more urban peers.

Rural schools differ systematically from urban and town schools, enjoying higher socioeconomic status, parental engagement and involvement, test scores beginning at school entry and extending throughout, and graduation rates. For the most part, these advantages place them above average, but below their suburban peers. These relative advantages are consistent over multiple measures, but they are not absolute.

While rural schools differ from other locales, they don't look the same across regions, as rural areas in the South and West differ dramatically from those in the Northeast and Midwest across a number of demographic and outcome measures. Like the descriptions of what "rural" is in the introduction, it's easier to describe how rural education contrasts to that in suburbs and cities than to describe what it looks like as a unified idea.

Rural schools face challenges, most of which are related to the lack of density and scale, that affect their nature and operations. These schools are small and thus have a hard time offering specialized programs, courses, services, and staff. These challenges are not going away, and in some areas, such as advanced course-taking, rural schools have found ways to offer their students alternative opportunities.

In other areas, solutions are harder to come by. Their remoteness brings infrastructure challenges that leave them behind the technological curve, especially in terms of Internet access and all the possibilities it has brought or will bring. This also leaves them with greater costs, such as transportation, which take up a higher percentage of the resources available to rural schools and districts. The challenges that come with minimal scale will remain, and rural schools will have to continue to find ways to make the most of their resources to serve students.

Despite these challenges, overall, rural schools and students enjoy many advantages. These may include headwinds from family structure, support, and involvement, and certainly include outcomes such as test scores across the board and the highest graduation rates across locales. Again, these average advantages are due in some part to the composition of rural schools. But that composition is not the whole story, as the gaps between demographic groups—gaps that prove to be large and stubborn in more urban areas—are smaller in rural areas.

This portrait captures the advantages and challenges rural education faces, and also shows how varied educational inputs and outputs are within the rural category. Such a broad context is essential grounding for considering the present and future of the education of rural students.

## NOTES

1  National Center for Education Statistics, "Locale Definitions and Criteria," accessed October 10, 2017, https://nces.ed.gov/programs/edge/docs/LOCALE_DEFINITIONS.pdf.

2  U.S. Census Bureau, "2010 Census Urban Area FAQs," last modified 2010, https://www.census.gov/geo/reference/ua/uafaq.html.

3  U.S. Census Bureau, "Metropolitan and Micropolitan," last modified January 11, 2017, https://www.census.gov/programs-surveys/metro-micro/about.html.

4  National Center for Education Statistics, "Early Childhood Surveys," accessed October 10, 2017, https://nces.ed.gov/nhes/surveytopics_early.asp.

5  National Center for Education Statistics, "Kindergarten Class of 2010–11 (ECLS—K:2011)," accessed October 10, 2017, https://nces.ed.gov/ecls/kindergarten2011.asp.

6  National Center for Education Statistics, "Rural Education in America," accessed October 10, 2017, https://nces.ed.gov/surveys/ruraled/tables/B.1.b.-1.asp.

7  Sean F. Reardon, Demetra Kalogrides, Andrew Ho, Ben Shear, Kenneth Shores, and Erin Fahle, "Stanford Education Data Archive," Stanford University Libraries, last modified 2016, http://purl.stanford.edu/db586ns4974.

8  U.S. Census Bureau, "How the Census Bureau Measures Poverty," last modified August 11, 2017, https://www.census.gov/topics/income-poverty/poverty/guidance/poverty-measures.html.

9  U.S. Department of Agriculture, "Income Eligibility Guidelines," last modified September 1, 2017, https://www.fns.usda.gov/school-meals/income-eligibility-guidelines.

10 U.S. Department of Education, "Civil Rights Data Collection (CRDC) for the 2013–14 School Year," last modified June 27, 2017, https://www2.ed.gov/about/offices/list/ocr/docs/crdc-2013-14.html.

11 Amber Noel, Patrick Stark, and Jeremy Redford, "Parent and Family Involvement in Education, from the National Household Education Surveys Program of 2012," National Center for Education Statistics, June 2016, https://nces.ed.gov/pubs2013/2013028rev.pdf.

12 National Center for Education Statistics, "Data Files," accessed October 10, 2017, https://nces.ed.gov/ccd/ccddata.asp.

13 National Center for Education Statistics, "NTPS Overview," accessed October 10, 2017, https://nces.ed.gov/surveys/ntps/overview.asp.

14 Soheyla Taie and Rebecca Goldring, "Characteristics of Public Elementary and Secondary Schools in the United States: Results from the 2015–16 National Teacher and Principal Survey First Look," National Center for Education Statistics, accessed December 7, 2017. https://nces.ed.gov/pubs2017/2017071.pdf.

15 Nat Malkus, "The AP Peak: Public Schools Offering Advanced Placement, 2000–12," American Enterprise Institute, accessed December 7, 2017. http://www.aei.org/wp-content/uploads/2016/01/The-AP-Peak.pdf.

16 Taie and Goldring, "Characteristics of Public Elementary and Secondary Schools in the United States," https://nces.ed.gov/pubs2017/2017071.pdf.

17 National Center for Education Statistics, "High School Longitudinal Study of 2009 (HSLS:09)," last modified May 2017, https://nces.ed.gov/surveys/hsls09/.

18 National Center for Education Statistics, "National Assessment of Educational Progress," last modified October 27, 2017, https://nces.ed.gov/nationsreportcard/.

19 U.S. Department of Education, "The ED*Facts* Initiative," last modified September 26, 2017, https://www2.ed.gov/about/inits/ed/edfacts/index.html.

20 Ibid.

21 National Center for Education Statistics, "High School Longitudinal Study of 2009."

22 U.S. Census Bureau, "American Community Survey (ACS)," accessed October 10, 2017, https://www.census.gov/programs-surveys/acs.html.

*Chapter 2*

# African-American Education in Rural Communities in the Deep South: "Making the Impossible Possible"

## Sheneka M. Williams

When compared to urban education, rural education has received little attention in the research literature. Moreover, much rural education research has been approached from a deficit perspective and has mostly examined the lives of white students living in rural America. But, as Nat Malkus points out in chapter 1 of this very volume, rural America is not a monolithic place.

In fact, rural America, which comprises approximately 51 million nonmetropolitan residents, spans from Native American communities in the West to small fishing villages in New England. Rural America also encompasses Midwestern farm towns with burgeoning Latino populations and African-American communities in the Deep South. Thus, rural America is vast, and diversity is increasing in the majority-white spaces.

Unfortunately, the research literature does not reflect this growing diversity. While there is a paucity of research that examines the schooling experiences and educational opportunity afforded to rural students in general, there is even less research that focuses specifically on the schooling of African-American students in the rural context. Although the number of African-American students who live in the rural South is relatively low when compared to the national school population, a significant number of African Americans live in the South. Therefore, it is important to understand and elucidate the educational and professional realities of students.

This is made doubly important because, although rural America is diversifying in terms of population, it is not necessarily diversifying in terms of wealth distribution. According to the U.S. Census Bureau's annual report, *Income and Poverty in the United States: 2013*, the official poverty rate in rural areas (persons living outside of metropolitan areas) was 16.1 percent, more than

1.5 percentage points higher than the national level. The poverty rate outside metro areas was down from 17.7 percent in 2012.[1]

The poverty rate is 30 percent greater in areas in which most Latino and African-American populations reside, which sheds light on the income inequalities that affect all aspects of the lives of disadvantaged students. Thus, low-skill and low-paying jobs in rural areas, combined with lower educational-attainment levels, are substantial factors in the rural income divergence—and, if left unaddressed, will widen opportunity gaps between students.

Thus, this chapter seeks to fill this gap by examining the educational opportunities afforded to African Americans who live in the rural South. It is important to examine the state of education for this population because they have been overlooked in policy discussions. More importantly, this research will add to the extant literature concerning rural education, thus providing policymakers with recommendations for how to narrow both the rural-education gap and the rural-income gap between whites and African Americans living in the rural South.

## THREE ERAS OF AFRICAN-AMERICAN EDUCATION IN THE RURAL SOUTH

Most scholars agree that educational opportunity considers inputs and outputs as related to students' schooling experiences. Inputs, for example, refer to teacher quality, curricular options, and student-assignment patterns, whereas outputs refer to college attendance and job attainment by recent graduates. James Coleman posited, "Education is a means to an end, and equal opportunity refers to later in life rather than the educational process itself."[2]

One reason the debate concerning equal educational opportunity continues is that "equal educational opportunity" cannot be standardized, and the phrase varies depending on how inputs are accessed by student populations. For example, students of a higher socioeconomic status (SES) have access to an array of educational opportunities relative to low-SES counterparts. That same claim manifests along racial lines. Thus, when one considers the intersection of being African American and poor, the threat of not receiving equal educational opportunity widens.

Moreover, residing in the rural South, being African American and living in poverty furthers the distance to equal educational opportunity. African Americans who live in the rural South often have a direct lineage to former slaves and a denial of public education. Thus, this chapter highlights three eras that have shaped educational opportunities for African-American students in the rural South: post-Reconstruction (1865–1954), post-*Brown* (1954–1980), and post-desegregation (1980–present).

The post-Reconstruction era was a time when African Americans were gaining freedom and ultimately citizenship in America. It was also a time in which the burgeoning movement for public education was taking place. Moreover, education sustained the population of freed blacks, as their "freedom," particularly in the South, was not immediate. Southern laws further oppressed African Americans from participating in the government; thus, black education developed in the context of political and economic oppression.[3]

Such political and economic oppression gave rise to a desire to become literate. Former slaves learned from other former slaves that becoming literate gave them a sense of pride and respect, and set a path for opportunity. Although some Northerners and a few Southern whites assisted, W. E. B. DuBois reminds us that "public education for all at public expense was, in the South, a Negro idea," which is important to bear in mind considering the historical landscape of educations for blacks, especially in the South.[4]

Just as free blacks fought for the right to be educated after slavery, the fight continued, yet in a different way after the landmark decision of *Brown v. Board of Education*. This case is significant in that it legally ended dejure segregation in public schools in the United States. Of course, while the Court handed down the decision in 1954, many districts in the South did not actually desegregate until twenty years later.

The long-standing segregation in U.S. schools, particularly in the South, emanated from the segregation of public places. Yet, the case was about more than race—as the case's premise, which focused on the inferiority of blacks, also included the segregation of resources. The Court ruled that "separate was inherently unequal," though many schools in the South remained segregated until the early 1970s.

The post-desegregation era is most often characterized by the peak moment in the late 1980s when the black–white achievement gap was most narrow, and evidence of resegregation of Southern schools shortly thereafter.[5] These developments led education researchers to study and debate further the factors related to student achievement outcomes. Moreover, scholars began to examine issues of race, social class, teacher quality, parent engagement, and so forth to determine why the achievement gap widened and why resegregation occurred.

While numerous studies have informed extant literature concerning educational opportunity for African-American students in urban contexts, very few studies have examined African-American students in the rural South. Moreover, a dearth of research has been conducted in rural contexts as compared to that of urban and suburban settings. Between 1991 and 2003, fewer than 500 articles were published on rural education[6]; however, this number has increased slightly thanks to journals such as the *Journal of Research in Rural Education*.

This chapter, then, seeks to enhance further rural-education literature. This chapter is undergirded by the theoretical framework of geography of opportunity, as place plays an important role in understanding the context in which this examination of rural education occurs. More importantly, this research examines black students in the Deep South—a topic that is almost void in any education literature.

## GEOGRAPHY OF OPPORTUNITY AND RURAL EDUCATION

According to the U.S. Census Bureau, "rural" spaces are those that are neither urbanized areas (consisting of 50,000 people or more) nor urbanized clusters (consisting of at least 2,500 people).[7] Despite the effects that many researchers associate with place, George C. Galster and Sean P. Killen contend that geography is not typically included in the definition of "equal educational opportunity" and further argue that inequalities based on geographic location can affect individual opportunities.[8]

The geographic distribution of opportunity is particularly important for families and children because it impacts children's schooling experiences. Schools in underserved communities, which are often racially and spatially isolated from opportunities, struggle to meet the needs of students from low-income neighborhoods.

Geography of opportunity has often been used in the social sciences to analyze the structural and individual aspects of opportunity. Within the past decade, it has been applied in education contexts to examine how place affects students' educational outcomes. Many of the decisions made about place, and specifically about rural spaces, are made in urban and/or metropolitan settings.

Thus, rural places are routinely more affected by place stratification—a model whereby some racial groups and places are situated in a hierarchy where "more advantaged groups seek to preserve social distance from less advantaged groups."[9] This is troubling, as place and space are very different along the urban–rural continuum, and because researchers increasingly recognize that access to opportunity is largely a function of geographical location, which accentuates the relationship between where one resides and existing opportunities.[10]

Galster and Killen coined the term "geography of opportunity" to analyze the structural and individual aspects of opportunity between neighborhoods.[11] Discriminatory policies, structural racism, and a history of government-sanctioned segregation led to the concentration of poverty in many urban cities today[12] and to inequitable distribution of opportunity by extension.[13]

Consequently, access to opportunity is often geographically clustered by neighborhood characteristics such as race and class, leaving many disadvantaged students without it. Scholars now document these patterns of inequality to accentuate that where people live affects their available opportunities.[14]

Moreover, the geographic dissemination of opportunity is especially important for children because of the implications it has for their schooling opportunities and educational outcomes, which are tied to economic outcomes, health, and overall well-being. In her book *Place, Not Race*, Sheryll Cashin used the geography of opportunity framework to elucidate how schools in underserved, underresourced communities—often racially and spatially insulated from opportunities—struggle to meet the needs of students from low-income neighborhoods.[15]

As such, many students matriculate into schools having very little exposure to the opportunities afforded to students from other neighborhoods. Some scholars have thus advocated for more comprehensive educational reforms that consider schools' social and community-based contexts when determining the equitable distribution of resources to high-needs schools.[16]

Geography of opportunity has also been examined in the context of advancements in science, technology, and transportation, with particular regard to the implications such advancements have for students' educational outcomes. William F. Tate IV, for example, used Geographic Information Systems (GIS) to map how advancements in biotechnology affected opportunities for students in neighborhoods where the advancement took place. He found that, in low-income neighborhoods in Detroit exposed to biotechnological advancement, only 33 percent of students received free and reduced lunch, compared to 66 percent for similar students not exposed to such advancement.

He also found that educational attainment increased for students in the former group and that they lived in higher-quality neighborhoods as evidenced by the significantly higher proportion of homes valued in the $100,000–$150,000 price range relative to students in the latter group. He concludes that students from low-income neighborhoods will continue to experience inequitable access to opportunities so long as opportunity and poverty remain spatially segregated along racial and class lines.[17]

Other scholars studying the geography of opportunity pay close attention to how communities of color, in particular, are often segregated from important opportunities such as access to adequate health care, safe neighborhoods, affordable housing, and sustainable employment.[18] These important elements of overall well-being have perpetuated the concentration of poverty in low-income neighborhoods, as inadequate access to opportunity continues the cyclical process of poverty. Further, inequitable geographies of opportunity are often associated with children's access to out-of-school contexts that support their academic, socioemotional, and cognitive development.

For instance, Korina M. Jocson and Elizabeth Thorne-Wallington mapped the location of literacy-rich environments in St. Louis,[19] which include "neighborhood assets like libraries, bookstores, community-based organizations, and museums."[20] They found that race, location of transportation routes, and median household income were all factors that predicted access and proximity to these opportunities that build students' development. Thus, in addition to school placement, disadvantaged students are further marginalized by inequitable access to the out-of-school supports that their nonmarginalized peers benefit from.

Poverty and geography-of-opportunity discussions typically center on the urban poor, particularly those in the inner city, while far less research and policy attention targets the rural poor. Consequently, poor residents in rural areas are frequently left behind, forgotten, and are not the targets of reforms to improve educational and economic outcomes in economically distressed communities throughout the country. Compared to metro areas, rural residents are more likely to live in neighborhoods where the proportion of people living in poverty is greater than 20 percent.

Further, the overall percentage of people living in poverty tends to be significantly higher in rural compared to metro areas. As such, increased policy attention must be devoted to the geography of opportunity in rural settings to better understand how and to what extent students are being marginalized in such settings.

## SOURCES

The experiences of African Americans in the rural South are more than just statistics on paper. Understanding the context in which these individuals grew up and the educational opportunities they were provided can lend a foundational base from which to better consider the geography of opportunity in rural contexts. Consider the narratives of three adult professionals who attended in rural school districts in the Deep South.

### Regional Context

The Deep South is a cultural and geographic subregion in the Southern United States. It is commonly referred to as the Cotton States, given that the production of cotton was a primary commodity crop.[21] The states most often include Georgia, Alabama, South Carolina, Mississippi, and Louisiana. Within each of these states, there are particular regions that are noted for their agricultural crops that were tended by slaves. Thus, the populations of these regions today are majority African American. These regions include the

Black Belt of Alabama, the Delta of Mississippi, and a lake community in Georgia. Thus, the narratives presented in this chapter capture the lived experiences of former students who represent each of the aforementioned areas.

## Black Belt of Alabama

Originally referred to the region's rich, black topsoil, the term "Black Belt" took on an additional meaning in the nineteenth century when the region was developed for cotton-plantation agriculture and the land worked by slaves. The sociological definition of the "Black Belt," as related to race, refers to a larger region of the Southern United State that stretches from Maryland to Texas, but centered on the Black Belt of upland areas of Georgia, Alabama, Mississippi, and Louisiana.

Wilcox County, Alabama, sits in the heart of the Black Belt region. A paper mill town, the median income for a household in the county is $16,646 and the median income for a family is $22,200. About 36 percent of families and 40 percent of the population live below the poverty line, including nearly 49 percent of those under age eighteen. The school district in Wilcox, Alabama, has a graduation rate of 87 percent, with 5 percent high schoolers proficient in high school math and 27 percent in English. In terms of education, 85 percent of whites complete high school and 23 percent complete college, compared to 73 percent and 8 percent, respectively, for blacks.

## The Mississippi Delta

The Mississippi Delta is the distinctive, northwest section of Mississippi, which lies between the Mississippi and Yazoo Rivers. The region has been called "The Most Southern Place on Earth," because of its unique racial, cultural, and economic history. The region was named as such because it attracted many speculators who developed land along the riverfronts for cotton plantations. They became wealthy farmers dependent on the labor of slaves, who comprised the vast majority of the population in these counties well before the Civil War, often twice the number of whites. Hence, today's population is majority black.

The population of Quitman County, Mississippi, is 7,761—48 percent male, 52 percent female. Black residents represent 70 percent of the county versus 28 percent for whites. The median income for the county is $24,583, with men making $26,599 to $16,619 for women. The median income for white residents is $41,187, compared to $23,400 for blacks. Quitman has a poverty rate of 40 percent, with 83 percent of blacks living in poverty to only 17 percent of whites. In terms of educational attainment, 74 percent of whites and 64 percent of blacks finish high school. Further, 19 percent of whites get college degrees, compared to only 10 percent of blacks.

Quitman County School District has a school population that is 52 percent male and 48 percent female. Further, the population is 95 percent black to about 1 percent white. Black students have a graduation rate of 78 percent, while no such statistics exist for white students in the district due to the limited sample size. In terms of reading achievement, 8 percent of males to 14 percent of females score proficiently on state tests, while only 10 percent of blacks do so to 29 percent of whites. In math, about 15 percent of both males and females score as proficient, while 14 percent of blacks to 19 percent of whites do so.

## Lake Community of Georgia

The lake communities of Georgia vary, but the lake community of Greene County is one of the most beautiful, yet most segregated places in the state. One side of the lake boasts million-dollar lakeside homes, while the other is occupied by black residents who fish and farm for a living. This juxtaposition furthers the economic and academic base of the community. Most recently, the area has become a playground for the rich and famous, with country singers and others holding big events at the Ritz Carlton Reynolds Plantation located in the area.

Greene County School District has a school population that is 52 percent black to about 32 percent white. The graduation rate for the district is 86 percent for blacks and 60 percent for whites. In terms of reading achievement, 41 percent of males to 23 percent of females score proficiently on state tests; only 49 percent of blacks score proficient compared to 76 percent of whites. In math, about 33 percent of males to 23 percent of females score proficient; roughly 72 percent of whites do so versus only 39 percent of blacks.

The three communities under study comprise majority black populations with high poverty rates. The schools in the districts exhibit low graduation rates, and student scores on national and state assessments lag behind others in the nation and each state. Thus, the narratives of participants who were educated in these locales can offer much to the larger discussion around the geography of opportunity and educational outcomes of students. More importantly, the narratives offered in this chapter provide balance to the quantitative discussion of black students educated in the rural South.

## CARL BOWEN'S STORY:
## "OVERCOMING CULTURAL NAIVETÉ"

Carl grew up in the heart of the Mississippi Delta, a land full of culture—though it often seems that people outside of the Delta lack an appreciation for the culture that exists there. That makes it difficult for local students to be noticed or appreciated by colleges and universities across the nation. Carl was a self-motivated, determined student and he wanted to take his foundational knowledge from the Delta and extend it into a broader context.

Carl's favorite subject was geography. He knew there was so much more to the world and how individuals from other places and ideologies fit into it. As a child, he would go on long hikes and bike rides into the country woods and follow along the railroads to explore nature. At night, his love for the solar system and the galaxy would lead him to search the clear sky for star formations. Carl understood the lack of access around him, so he took the precious gems of the earth and developed a liking for physical geography. This led him to study atmospheric science in college and build a career as a physical scientist.

Although Carl went to a prestigious university for black males, the encouragement to do so did not necessarily come from his parents or teachers. Both of his parents attended community college, and they didn't "push" a particular direction on their sons. Instead, the motivation came from within. Carl left his hometown and attended a parochial high school in St. Louis, Missouri, seeking access to the vast opportunities afforded to students in other schools. It was more than curriculum; he wanted to meet other people. He was able to go to school with whites, Koreans, Asians, and so forth. In essence, he wanted to "overcome cultural naiveté," as he noted that everything was so segregated in his hometown.

Having lived in a few large cities across the United States, Carl is hoping to settle in the Deep South in the near future. He admits that he is not quite ready to return home, but when he does, he intends to teach at the local community college. He desires to share his love for geography with local students. Moreover, he wants to share the lived experiences of traveling and working abroad and encountering other cultures with students in the Delta. He believes that hearing from one of their own will instill the drive to compete globally and lessen the threat of cultural naiveté.

## RICHARD PETTUS'S STORY:
## "I CAN GET THERE FROM RIGHT HERE"

Richard grew up in Greene County, Georgia, on the outskirts of Greensboro. When he attended, he went to a comprehensive high school that offered a "dual-seal" (college prep and vocational) diploma. He attained both, which afforded him the opportunity to take advanced placement classes and compete in electrical wiring competitions. His high school also embraced students from another district so that those students would have educational opportunities at the secondary level. Richard carries that same spirit of helping others reach their goal. He intends to take that influence to another level; his career ambition is to serve as a university president.

Richard was not always a model student—though his math teacher, Ms. Hemmings, pushed him to become one. He began to fall in love with math when she took away his recess until he completed multiple upper-level math worksheets. He did not understand it at the time, but his teacher saw his mathematical abilities. She then began to give him the same opportunities that two white boys received—no recess, but math enrichment instead. His love for math never ceased, and Richard pursued an undergraduate degree in business because he believed that he could do it.

Although Richard's parents did not attend college, they emphasized the necessity of a college degree to all their children. They also never let an opportunity pass to let him know that he could "get to anywhere I want to be from right where I am." To him, the phrase simply meant his parents believed that he could be successful coming from a small town, and that he should be proud to be born and raised in Greene County, Georgia.

They were not able to provide any knowledge about the process or experience as Richard started applying for schools, but they found others who could assist their children. One of whom was Richard's high school guidance counselor, Mr. Beasley. Mr. Beasley looked out for Richard and would often get him out of in-school suspension and talk to him about college and other life lessons. Richard and Mr. Beasley keep in touch still today, and the mentoring sessions continue.

Richard, on the whole, is still very connected with his community. Living only thirty minutes away, he runs a foundation in his local community. The school system is more segregated than when he attended school; therefore, he uses his foundation to close the gaps that have been widened by the effects of segregation. For example, his philanthropic endeavors provide seminars that assist students with financial aid, mentoring, college tours, ACT/SAT waivers, family budgets, health awareness, and spiritual guidance. The work that he does, whether in higher education or in the community, allows him to have a broader perspective about what "success" means to students.

Richard is very proud of the community that helped to raise him. In fact, going home is nostalgic for Richard. He even recalls how the racist incidents now make him feel humbled and grateful for the covering and guidance of God, his ancestors, and those who saw greater in him. Although his hometown is more segregated now than when he lived there, he remains inspired.

## DENISE RAYLE'S STORY:
## "MAKING THE IMPOSSIBLE POSSIBLE"

Denise Rayle attended school in Wilcox County, Alabama, at one time considered one of the poorest counties in the country. Regardless, Denise did not let that deter her from aiming higher. Sharing a love for both English and math, Denise began to read and write creatively at an early age. She also became fascinated with multiplication tables and solving for the "unknown." That creative curiosity led Denise to finish high school and attend the state's flagship university on a Coca-Cola Foundation Scholarship. She went on to graduate from college as one of the first African-American women to receive a bachelor's degree in physics from that university. Today, Denise works as a rocket scientist with NASA, and she is her local town's example of "hidden figures."

Born to a single mother who was a first-generation college student, Denise knew that she would attend college. She grew up in very poor school district that rarely had textbooks and that did not offer after-school programs for enrichment. However, the teachers in the schools never missed a beat; they never stopped teaching the curriculum, nor did they cease teaching the students to dream. This made them feel like they had everything—often compelling them to compete in regional spelling bees, science fairs, and math competitions.

Participating in regional and state competitions prepared Denise for later competition in college. She did not feel inferior at the large state university, but she did find it somewhat difficult to match up to her classmates in certain advanced and honors classes during her freshman year. She realized that other students had already taken most of the advanced calculus and chemistry classes in high school, while she had only taken precalculus, the highest math course her school offered. Therefore, Denise simultaneously attended a nearby junior college and her four-year university in order to catch up. This helped her to be a bit more competitive during her first college years.

Now, as she reflects on her career and the educational opportunity she received in Wilcox, she realizes that opportunities, in general, still lag there. The school district is still very much behind in terms of subjects offered to other students throughout the state. Some schools still struggle with full Internet access, including in students' homes, and jobs and economic growth remain limited. Because of these access gaps, Denise worries whether students are getting the resources and teaching necessary to compete globally.

Therefore, she returns home as often as she can to talk about how her interest in STEM subjects changed her life and career trajectory. Currently, Denise is looking at ways to create an online network of STEM professionals that students can access, learn from, and ask questions about their homework and STEM careers. As she states it, "I want them to see examples of science and math in their everyday experiences so that they will be motivated to imagine impossible possibilities."

## LESSONS LEARNED

Similar characteristics emanate from these three narratives; however, the overarching theme that encompasses their trajectory is "making the impossible possible." Each individual indicated a desire to further their knowledge base and cultural understanding beyond their home community. They endorsed struggles that resulted from the effects of being isolated from opportunity, while being self-motivated to better themselves by attending college and furthering their education and opportunity landscape.

For example, Carl was aware that his school had a limited curriculum. He shared, "I asked my parents to allow me to go live with my aunt so that I could attend a more challenging school." He also suggested, "I didn't even participate in my high school graduation. I didn't see it as special. I knew I would go farther, so I wanted to wait and celebrate those loftier accomplishments." This accentuates the dynamic relationship between isolation from opportunity and self-motivation to overcome in spite of adversary common in many African Americans the rural South.

In addition to motivating themselves, participants added that their teachers played a huge role in their successes. Two of the three participants named teachers who encouraged them to challenge themselves and achieve in certain subjects. For example, Richard noted that a teacher realized his mathematical abilities and therefore kept him in from recess to train in higher-level math. To this day, Richard keeps in touch with her and other teachers and mentors in the community. Denise also mentioned that her English, math, and physics teachers saw abilities within her that she did not notice herself. The teachers did not view them within a framework of deficiency—something commonplace in rhetoric surrounding rural education—and this had a substantial impact.

The narratives also expressed participants' desire to give back to their respective communities—whether they returned there to live or not. All three intend to leverage their abilities to share with their home communities. For example, Richard shared, "I currently have a non-profit organization. We help the youth reach their educational level of success by not only helping them, but also by assisting their family better support the youth." Another participant, Carl, included, "I intend to retire back home and teach at the local community college. I want to share my passion of geography and physics with future generations."

Although most rural towns are separated from many educational and economic opportunities, close-knit ties and familial values rest within those who grow up there.[22] Therefore, it is no surprise that the data reveal a willingness to reach back and assist others who do not know how or where to access assistance. Thus, the findings highlight that even though educational opportunities are sparse in rural contexts, some overcome barriers through self-motivation and community support.

## MOVING THE CONVERSATION FORWARD

In order to sufficiently redress the economic, educational, and professional realities faced by African Americans living in the rural South, tangible actions in both the academic and policymaking arenas must be employed to ensure that these students are better served through schooling. Researchers, in particular, are prominent actors on this front and have a professional obligation to shed light on the challenges African-American students face in rural contexts, as well as the processes by which many have overcome them.

Further research surrounding rural education must reflect the diversity of culture and experiences represented in those contexts. As such, this chapter hopes to inspire the research community to further expend the requisite time and resources into a more inclusive analysis of contemporary rural education that features both the economic and educational challenges highlighted by this volume and commensurate success stories that accentuate the spirit of "making this impossible possible."

The latter is especially important, as researchers are uniquely positioned to shape discourse and policy decisions surrounding rural education. As much of the research focused on rural contexts has approached rural education from a deficit mind-set, discourse surrounding students residing in the South has often assumed a position of integrity among them. What if researchers deconstructed the narratives about rural education, understanding students instead as fully capable of excelling in their education as illustrated the stories shared in this chapter?

Might this infuse passion and action among policymakers to divert resources to support and align well with the spirit of triumph that is vibrant among rural residents, especially within the African-American community? The hope here is that researchers will take advantage of their unique positions as storytellers and knowledge creators, and ensure that the voices of marginalized students are heard and their commitment to academic excellence "in spite of circumstance" is celebrated.

Policymakers, too, play an important part in remedying the condition of rural education. They must respond to the stories and research that scholars are beginning to make available and utilize their positions to support the efforts of those advocating for greater investment into rural education. This includes taking steps to ensure that extant disparities between and within the rural context, particularly along racial and socioeconomic lines, are remedied.

Policymakers can leverage the culture, history, and spirit of resilience endorsed by African Americans in the rural South to support initiatives that encourage highly qualified teachers and administrators to seek employment in these contexts. Such initiatives would elucidate where policymakers stand on the issue to support the educational and economic plight of African-American students in the rural South.

To reiterate, we must do more and better research: Rural schools are understudied, and the experiences of African-American students and communities, in particular, are almost entirely absent. Much work remains to be done before our understanding of history and policy of and in these areas are adequate.

And we must also move away from a deficit mind-set. Rural communities, and particularly African-American rural communities, are rich in resources: culture, history, community, and so forth. If we focused policy on trying to maximize and leverage those resources rather than simply managing a population of people we don't wish to understand, we would be much more likely to meet with success.


## CONCLUSION

As I reflect on the process of writing this chapter, I am reminded of my own schooling experiences and access to educational opportunities. I, too, am a product of a small, rural district in the Deep South. Although I am a third-generation college student, I realize that I am an outlier in the rural African-American context, as are the narratives presented in this chapter. It is important, though, to share narratives that counter the deficit perspectives that often permeate rural education and the education of African Americans, in general. Somewhere at the intersection of both, there are exemplars of "making the impossible possible."

Following the work of scholars such as Cashin and others, this work indicates how schools in underserved, underresourced communities—often racially and spatially insulated from opportunities—struggle to meet the needs of students from low-income neighborhoods.[23] Thus, while this chapter highlights students who prevailed against the odds, it also displays a need for researchers and policymakers to better understand how place, as it relates to the educational opportunity of rural students, plays a role in the outcomes of students who live there.

This is particularly important as approximately 20 percent of the nation's school population exists in rural areas. The participants in this study grew up in districts and towns in which poverty, segregation, and limited access to resources are the norm. While many scholars, myself included, have researched and argued that one's zip code in urban areas should not determine students' access to opportunity, the same is true for students in rural areas. In the end, this chapter calls for expansion of research in educational opportunity, as African-American students educated in rural contexts have been neglected in research.

## NOTES

1 Lorin Kusmin, *Rural America at a Glance, 2012 Edition* (Washington, DC: U.S. Department Agriculture, Economic Research Service, 2012).

2 James S. Coleman, "What Is Meant by 'An Equal Educational Opportunity'?" *Oxford Review of Education* 1, no. 1 (1975), 28.

3 James D. Anderson, *The Education of Blacks in the South, 1860–1935* (Chapel Hill: University of North Carolina Press, 1988).

4 Ibid., 6.

5 Gary Orfield and John T. Yun, *Resegregation in American Schools* (Cambridge, MA: The Civil Rights Project, Harvard University, 1999), https://escholarship.org/content/qt6d01084d/qt6d01084d.pdf; and Erica Frankenberg and Gary Orfield, *The Resegregation of Suburban Schools* (Cambridge, MA: Harvard Education Press, 2012).

6 Michael L. Arnold et al., "A Look at the Condition of Rural Education Research," *Journal of Research in Rural Education* 20, no. 6 (2005), 1–25.

7 U.S. Census Bureau, "Geography: Reference," 2015, https://www.census.gov/geo/reference/.

8 George C. Galster and Sean P. Killen, "The Geography of Metropolitan Opportunity: A Reconnaissance and Conceptual Framework," *Housing Policy Debate* 6, no. 1 (1995), 7–43.

9 John R. Logan and Richard D. Alba, "Locational Returns to Human Capital: Minority Access to Suburban Community Resources," *Demography* 30, no. 2 (1993), 244.

10 Terrance L. Green, "Places of Inequality," *Urban Review* 47, no. 4 (November 2015), 717–41; and William F. Tate IV, "'Geography of Opportunity': Poverty, Place, and Educational Outcomes," *Educational Researcher* 37, no. 7 (2008), 397–411.

11 Galster and Killen, "Geography of Metropolitan Opportunity."

12 Richard Rothstein, *The Color of Law: A Forgotten History of How Our Government Segregated America* (New York: Liveright, 2017).

13 Myron Orfield, "Politics and Regionalism," in *Urban Sprawl: Causes, Consequences, & Policy Responses*, ed. Gregory D. Squires (Washington, DC: Urban

Institute Press, 2002), 237–54; John A. Powell, Jason Reece, and Samir Gambhir, *The Geography of Opportunity: Austin Region* (Columbus, OH: Kirwan Institute, 2007), http://greendoors.org/docs/opportunity_mapping/Austin_Opportunity_Report.pdf; and Edward W. Soja, *Seeking Spatial Justice* (Minneapolis: University of Minnesota Press, 2010).

14  Green, "Places of Inequality"; Xavier Briggs, ed., *The Geography of Opportunity: Race and Housing Choice in Metropolitan America* (Washington, DC: Brookings Institution Press, 2006); and Tate, "Geography of Opportunity."

15  Sheryll Cashin, *Place, Not Race: A New Vision of Opportunity in America* (Boston, MA: Beacon Press, 2015).

16  Jennifer Jellison Holme and Virginia Snodgrass Rangel, "Putting School Reform in Its Place: Social Geography, Organizational Social Capital, and School Performance," *American Educational Research Journal* 49, no. 2 (2012), 257–83; Sonya Douglass Horsford and Julian Vasquez Heilig, "Community-Based Education Reform in Urban Contexts: Implications for Leadership, Policy, and Accountability," *Urban Education* 49, no. 8 (2014), 867–70; Peter M. Miller, Tanya Brown, and Rodney Hopson, "Centering Love, Hope, and Trust in the Community: Transformative Urban Leadership Informed by Paulo Freire," *Urban Education* 46, no. 5 (2011), 1078–99; H. Richard Milner IV, "Analyzing Poverty, Learning, and Teaching through a Critical Race Theory Lens," *Review of Research in Education* 37, no. 1 (2013), 1–53; Pedro A. Noguera and Lauren Wells, "The Politics of School Reform: A Broader and Bolder Approach for Newark," *Berkeley Review of Education* 2, no. 1 (January 2011), 5–25; and Mark Warren, "Communities and Schools: A New View of Urban Education Reform," *Harvard Educational Review* 75, no. 2 (2005), 133–73.

17  Tate, "Geography of Opportunity."

18  Briggs, *The Geography of Opportunity*; Peter Drier, John Mollenkopf, and Todd Swanstrom, *Place Matters: Metropolitics for the 21st Century*, 3rd ed. (Lawrence: University Press of Kansas, 2014); and Powell, Reece, and Gambhir, *The Geography of Opportunity*.

19  Korina M. Jocson and Elizabeth Thorne-Wallington, "Mapping Literacy-Rich Environments: Geospatial Perspectives on Literacy and Education," *Teachers College Record* 115, no. 6 (2013), 1–24.

20  Green, "Places of Inequality," 8.

21  Theda Perdue, *Race and the Atlanta Cotton States Exposition of 1895* (Athens: University of Georgia Press, 2011).

22  Mara Casey Tieken, *Why Rural Schools Matter* (Chapel Hill: University of North Carolina Press, 2014).

23  Cashin, *Place, Not Race*.

*Chapter 3*

# From Basketball to Overdose Capital: The Story of Rural America, Schools, and the Opioid Crisis

Clayton Hale and Sally Satel

The year 2006 saw quite the upset for high school basketball in West Virginia. After securing a winning streak years in the making, the Ravenswood Red Devils finished up the season with only a single loss and took home their first West Virginia State AA Championship Title.[1] After beating the Keyser Golden Tornados 49–46, the Red Devils faced the Logan Wildcats in the state semifinals.[2] The Wildcats were defending the state title and had just emerged from a 75–49 win over the Mt. View Golden Knights.[3] The stakes were high in Ravenswood, but the Red Devils emerged victorious, a single basket securing their victory: 64–62.

The Red Devils' upset over the Logan Wildcats cleared the way for the team's victory in the finals over Bluefield High. Yet, back in Logan, another upset of far greater significance was in the making for the state of West Virginia and the nation: In 2006, Logan County, West Virginia, unseated the city of Baltimore, Maryland, as the county with the highest opioid overdose rate in the country.[4]

Unlike the Logan Wildcats' narrow defeat in the state semifinals, there was virtually no contest, as Logan County more than doubled Baltimore's overdose rate for the year.[5] Despite the overdose rate in Baltimore increasing by more than a third since 2006, the city has never reclaimed its former position, as counties across Appalachia easily clinched the top spot. In 2015, McDowell County, West Virginia—the self-proclaimed "basketball capital of the United States"—recorded a staggering overdose rate of 126.0 deaths per 100,000.[6]

In the period following World War II, places like McDowell Co. and much of rural America became defined by the local high school and, in particular, school sports.[7] But, today, the symbol of the Ravenswood Red Devil—a menacing visage of a horned devil—has been supplanted by that of an over-dosed mom slumped over in the front seat of her car in a Walmart parking lot. As the situation intensifies, local communities have been forced to divert their attention away from fielding championship teams to ensuring that their first responders and school nurses are equipped with naloxone, the opioid-overdose reversal drug.[8]

The opioid epidemic has been years in the making, percolating just beneath the surface of national attention until finally breaking through with a vengeance. As the opioid crisis continues to devastate rural America, the local county schools—long a beacon of stability in small towns—struggle to anchor their communities. Increasingly, this means that schools are having to confront the bitter realities of drug abuse and addiction among their own students and families. The local schoolhouse has always been key to under-standing rural life, and for understanding the opioid crisis it is no exception.

## THE MAKINGS OF A CRISIS

In 2016, an estimated 42,249 opioid overdoses occurred in the United States—a figure mirroring the number of deaths from car crashes and nearly three times that of gun homicides.[9] With the overdose rate for the nation top-ping just over 13 deaths per 100,000 in 2016—over ten times the rate at the peak of the heroin crisis in the mid-1970s—public-health officials describe the situation as an *epidemic*, a term generally reserved for a sharp rise in residents affected by infectious outbreaks.

The term "opioid" refers to narcotic prescription medications, such as oxy-codone (the narcotic in Percocet and OxyContin) and hydrocodone (Vicodin), as well as heroin and synthetic drugs such as fentanyl, which is 25 to 50 times as potent as heroin. Unlike drug epidemics of the past, rural America has found itself at the center of the current crisis with states like West Virginia, New Hampshire, Ohio, and Kentucky maintaining the highest rates of fatal opioid overdoses in the nation.

The roots of the crisis can be traced to the early 1990s when physicians, responding to pressure from patient advocates and some in the medical com-munity, began to prescribe opioid painkillers more liberally to treat pain. Aggressive marketing by narcotic manufacturers further abetted this practice. In 1995, the American Pain Society recommended that pain be assessed as the "fifth vital sign"—along with the standard four (blood pressure, temperature, pulse, and respiratory rate). With such strong winds from the medical com-munity, it did not take long for the clouds to set in over the rust belt and rural Appalachia.

A relatively unhealthy population with insurance—many of whom had spent their entire lives working as manual labor and smoking cigarettes—primed the region for both chronic and cancer-related pain. A devastated economy caused largely by the mass exodus of manufacturing and coal-mining jobs exacerbated the problem by introducing new financial, cultural, and social pain. Pills flooded the region—so much so that OxyContin came to be known as "hillbilly heroin," because when the pill was crushed, it could be snorted or injected to provide a superior high that was pharmacologically pure.

Much of the problem had to do with the sheer number of opioids that entered circulation. Research demonstrates that pain patients who are prescribed opioids for legitimate pain management are not at a great risk of developing an opioid addiction, unless they have a prior problem with addiction or suffer from a mental illness.[10] But when prescribed a month's supply of opioids for a tooth ache or minor surgery, these patients would take a few and then stash the rest in the medicine cabinet only to later be stolen or given away to a friend or relative—the way most teenagers who abuse painkillers obtain their pills.[11]

As the number of opioids in circulation began to increase, so too did deaths from opioid painkillers, peaking in 2011. By then, most states had begun to crack down on the number of prescriptions and shutter pill mills; however, reducing the number of those addicted on these pills was not so easy. In recent years, many of these addicts have found their way to illicit opioids: heroin smuggled in from Mexico and fentanyl, a powerful synthetic opioid, mainly obtained through illicit channels from China. Overdoses from these synthetic opioids have skyrocketed, having more than doubled nationally in just one year to 19,413 overdoses in 2016, according to data from the CDC.

Here it is important to provide a bit of context. A broader rise in mortality among the white working class, a trend to which many of these drug deaths belong, has been underway for quite some time in rural America, denoting a crisis beyond a mere drug epidemic—what Princeton economists Sir Angus Deaton and his wife Anne Case appropriately label as "deaths of despair."[12]

In this sense, the opioid epidemic can be understood to be symptomatic of a cultural and social upheaval as well as a public health crisis. Rather than tackling this problem in its entirety, what follows is an examination of one often overlooked component of the crisis: the role of schools and the education system.

## PRICE PAID BY CHILDREN OF ADDICTS

School principals, like many small-town civic leaders, read their local paper. The prospect of a student being featured as the athlete of the month is generally enough motivation to skim the headlines. Tracy LeMasters of Cottageville Elementary School in West Virginia has found herself doing so for a different reason: to check if any of her students' parents have been arrested for drug possession. She hopes that with a bit of warning, her teachers and the part-time school counselor might be ready to handle any spillover into class from a recent arrest.

Middle-of-the-night encounters between law enforcement and drug users with children have become so common in West Virginia that the state, through its Children's Justice Task Force, launched a program—Handle with Care—to give police officers responding to a call the night before a direct line of communication with the school the next morning.[13] The process is simple: if a child is exposed to violence, trauma, or criminal activity, a letter listing the time the incident occurred as well as the name of the child is sent to school. From there, school officials attempt to provide the additional care the child may need.

While stories of overdoses dominate local reporting, many of the epidemic's casualties are not the users themselves, but rather their children, forced to face the consequences of their parent's use. While the exact number of children living with a parent who uses opioids is unknown, the 2009 *National Survey on Drug Use and Health* (NSDUH) estimated that between 2002 and 2007, 2.1 million children under the age of eighteen lived with a parent who was dependent on or abused illicit drugs.[14]

Living with a parent who abuses drugs is likely to have profound implications for a child's future success and development. It is well documented that the children of illicit drug users are not only at an increased risk of abuse and neglect, but also of developing social, emotional, and behavioral disorders.[15] Further, while the association between parental substance abuse and a child's cognitive development is less well established, research suggests that parental substance abuse is associated with poorer child academic performance.[16]

Many effects of parental drug use on children cannot be traced back to a specific disorder or condition but might help to explain certain behaviors. For example, some children of opioid users act out in school, not because they have a behavioral condition, but out of a simple desire to stay at school rather than return home.[17] While the school day might function as a sanctuary for the child, for their parents it can serve as an opportunity to use while the children are away.[18]

The consequences of illicit opioid use can quickly become dire, and it is the children, tragically, who are often the ones to witness such parents at their breaking points. Frantic calls to 911 from a child whose parent will not wake up or scenes of parents passed out in the front seat of the car with the child in the rear are now becoming all too familiar. As first responders struggle to revive the parents with naloxone, rush them off to the hospital, or roll them off to the morgue, their children suffer the consequences.

Law enforcement on the scene often must step up to do their best to play parent until a caretaker, be it a relative or a social worker, can be found. Such a task often entails officers filling in as makeshift trauma counselors or even—as one story in the *Washington Post* noted—just as someone to sign a child's math homework due the next day.[19]

In a paper for Princeton's *The Future of Children* project, Diana Kronstadt provides a few numbers to understand the impact on newborns whose parents fail to get clean. Kronstadt cites work by Judy Howard and her colleagues at UCLA conducted throughout the 1980s. "By their first birthday," they wrote, "48 percent of infants of untreated heroin users were living with their biological parents. But by the time the children reached preschool ages, only 9 percent of children of untreated heroin users were still cared for by their biologic mother."[20]

While these figures have most likely changed a bit since then, the finding echoes today wherein the opioid epidemic has displaced thousands of children whose parents were swallowed by the wave of addiction that has flooded the country. Since 2012, the number of children in foster care across the country has increased by 10 percent to 437,465 in 2016. Further, the percentage of removals where parental substance use was cited as a contributing factor rose to 34 percent in 2016, a 17 percent increase from 2012.

This figure, however, is likely an undercount, as many substance use cases are classified under the larger umbrella of parental "neglect."[21] In just one state, Vermont, the number of children in state care increased by a staggering 75 percent from 2014 to 2015, and opioids were involved in 80 percent of the cases in which children under three were placed in state care.[22]

As mothers and fathers go missing, relatives, often grandparents, are forced to step in. In 2012, the Census Bureau estimated that 2.7 million grandparents were raising their grandchildren and 39 percent had been doing so for five or more years.[23] It's a formidable undertaking, even in situations where a parent is gone for only a brief period of time. For example, in states such as New Hampshire, Kentucky, Vermont, and West Virginia—where the epidemic has been particularly harsh—family members who are not the child's legal guardian are barred from enrolling the child in school or even signing off on a report card.[24]

In rural areas, this can mean driving miles to the next county because relatives cannot enroll the child in their local district. Many of these states also limit the ability of relatives to make medical decisions for the child. In more extreme situations, a new generation of "opioid orphans"—children who have lost their parents to opioids—are having to be relocated hundreds of miles away from their homes, plucked out of school as states struggle to find eligible foster parents nearby.[25]

Beyond the toll on families, immense pressure is placed on state resources as budgets are pushed to the brink. In Ohio, for example, spending on placement costs for children taken into state custody has risen by 20 percent since 2013 to $331 million in 2016, driven predominantly by drug-related cases.[26] As state and local budgets continue to come under pressure, spending on economic development and education is often first to be cut to balance the ledger.[27] Beyond merely a grim fiscal future for many states, time, attention, and personal resources of many public servants, particularly educators, are being diverted from other pressing matters.

Principal LeMasters, mentioned earlier, captured this reality rather well. When asked on *PBS News Hour* in 2016 what impact the opioid crisis has had on her school—where she has estimated that nearly a third of students do not live with their biological parents due to drug abuse—she replied, "We assume that everything needs to be provided here. So that means, if they need clothes, we're going to give them clothes. If they need food, we're going to get them food. You know, they need love, we're giving them the hug."[28]

## SUBSTANCE USE AMONG STUDENTS

Hunter Burkey was just about to begin his senior year at Belpre High School on the border of southeast Ohio and West Virginia, when he died from a heroin overdose. Burkey was a member of the high school football team, sang in the church choir, and was always keen to give out a warm embrace to anyone who needed one. A "bad" batch of heroin had been making its way through the Ohio valley around the time of Hunter's death, reports indicated, yet his grandfather was quick to comment that "there is no such thing as 'good' heroin."

The seventeen-year-old's death is a stark reminder that not even our nation's youth are beyond the reach of the current epidemic. As his aunt so bluntly put it, "Hunter was a strong child; he was a smart child. He tried something and it killed him."[29]

In 2016, an estimated 4.8 percent of all high school seniors had misused an opioid in the past year and 1.7 percent had used one in the past thirty days, according to the Monitoring the Future Survey ("misuse" refers to use in any way not directed by a doctor—in short, anything from taking one pill obtained from a friend, to daily use of nonprescribed medication, to addiction).[30] Luckily, the figures for heroin for the same cohort are much lower at 0.3 percent for annual use and 0.2 percent for past thirty-day use.

Although annual opioid use among twelfth graders has been declining since 2009, before then, use had increased dramatically from 1992 to 1994.

Annual nonmedical use of opioid painkillers for twelfth graders tripled from 3.3 percent in 1992 to 9.5 percent in 2004, as the availability of such drugs increased nationally. By 2010, a staggering 54.2 percent of all twelfth graders nationwide indicated that it would be "fairly easy" to obtain opioids.[31]

Fortunately, mirroring a concurrent decline in use, the opioid overdose rate for adolescents in high school has remained relatively modest. However, overdoses increase dramatically in the years following high school. In 2016, the overdose rates among seventeen-year-olds were only 2.0 deaths per 100,000; however, for eighteen- and nineteen-year-olds, these rates increase to 3.9 and 6.7 deaths per 100,000, respectively. By age twenty-five the overdose rate more than triples to 22.3 deaths per 100,000.[32] These figures suggest, in part, that the transition from school life to adulthood marks a crucial juncture for determining future opioid use.

Rural and small-town adolescents are found to have a higher prevalence of opioid "misuse" as well as a younger age of first use than their urban peers.[33] The reasons for this are not entirely understood.

While rural adolescents are more likely to be exposed to certain protective social and community factors compared to their urban counterparts, such as lower peer substance use for other drugs and stronger religious beliefs, these factors exist alongside higher rates of criminal involvement among rural adolescents, lower perceived risk of opioids, and an increased use of the emergency room for medical treatment, where opioids are likely to be dispensed.[34] Rural youth are most likely to obtain opioids through diversion—either stealing or receiving from friends and family—they are also more likely, relative to their urban peers, to obtain opioids from a drug dealer or from the medical system.[35]

In contrast to many other illicit drugs—notably cannabis—opioids are often perceived by rural Americans not only as a low-risk drug, but sometimes even acceptable due to their strong association with the medical community.[36] This unique relationship, along with high rates of use in rural America, means that opioids are relatively abundant in rural areas. The ample supply has enabled painkillers to be used in barter exchanges. In areas where poverty is prevalent and public or private assistance is scarce, opioids, particularly OxyContin, can serve as a form of currency—a lifeline, used to purchase food, clothes, and even dental care, with Medicaid or another means of insurance picking up the majority of the tab.[27]

## DRUG EDUCATION, DRUG-FREE AND RECOVERY HIGH SCHOOLS, AND THE JUVENILE JUSTICE SYSTEM

As the opioid epidemic continues to intensify, schools are fighting on the front lines of both response and prevention efforts. Beyond occupying a substantial share of a child's day, schools are a natural site for establishing and enforcing safe attitudes regarding drug use, as well as a prime location to teach and disseminate essential information about the risks of opioids.

Moreover, the local school serves as a key institution for orienting the lives of those around it. Research has suggested that strong bonds to one's school can itself lower an adolescent's odds of abusing opioids by exerting a form of positive peer pressure to conform to a drug-free norm.[38] Schools alone will not solve the crisis, but there is much they can do.

First and foremost, schools can teach about the dangers and harms associated with opioids. As noted earlier, particularly in rural areas, there is often a misperception surrounding the safety of opioids. As Maryland's Lt. Gov. Boyd K. Rutherford has put it, "Virtually every third grader can tell you that cigarettes are bad for you, but most don't know that taking someone else's prescription drugs is harmful."[39] Recognizing the importance of education efforts, states like Ohio and New York have passed laws requiring that schools include opioid-abuse prevention as part of their health education curriculum.[40]

Schools are also working alongside the juvenile justice system to help teens with drug problems. A key component of this collaboration is partnerships between schools and juvenile drug courts that provide treatment to eligible, drug-involved juvenile offenders with the ultimate goal of preventing future substance abuse and encounters with the legal system. Through use of court-mandated incentives and sanctions, juvenile drug courts can carefully monitor students with prior drug offenses to make sure they are present for the school day, complete assignments, engage with both teachers and parents, and participate in activities that enhance future employment prospects.[41]

While, in theory, the relationship between juvenile drug courts and schools benefits everyone involved, schools often lack the resources to give these students extra attention. In these situations, one alternative to traditional schools is specially designated "recovery" high schools. These offer a unique opportunity for student users to remain drug free by combining treatment and counseling services within a drug-free environment. Mostly, students who attend do so voluntarily, but some are court-ordered.

Research suggests that these schools are effective in reducing substance use. Using a survey of 321 students in seventeen recovery high schools, Paul Moberg of the University of Wisconsin and Andrew J. Finch of Vanderbilt University found that reports of at least weekly use of alcohol, cannabis, or other illicit drugs were reduced from 90 percent in the twelve months before entering the school to 7 percent at the time of the survey.[42]

One promising example is Hope Academy in Indianapolis, Indiana, the last stop on Secretary of Education Betsy DeVos's "Rethink Schools" tour last September.[43] Hope Academy operates as a charter school and raises additional funds in order to provide their services tuition-free. Students are expected to attend eight classes a day, as they would in any other high school; the difference is that their classes include core concepts of rehabilitation.[44] In addition to these classes, Hope Academy also provides regular treatment and drug-counseling services.

Although a promising option, there are only forty or so recovery high schools across the country, with a handful servicing rural areas.[45] Clearly, more are needed.

Another intriguing arena for future interventions is school sports. A study published in the *American Journal of Public Health* from Philip Veliz and his colleagues at the University of Michigan, analyzing the Monitoring the Future Survey, found that adolescent participants in high-injury sports had 50 percent higher odds of nonmedical opioid use than adolescents who did not participate in these types of sports.[46] Yet, another study from the same researchers a few years later published in the journal *Pediatrics* found that participation in safer sports and exercise may decrease the odds of heroin or nonmedical use of opioids among adolescents.[47]

Finally, research published in 2017 found that, in general, there was no difference between twelfth graders who participated in sports and twelfth graders who did not participate in sports. However, consistent with the findings made earlier, students participating in ice hockey or weightlifting were found to have higher odds of opioid misuse while those participating in basketball or track had lower odds.[48] More research is needed in order to establish a clear relationship between various athletics and opioid misuse.

Lastly, schools are beginning to combine the advantages of an activity that might encourage teens to remain drug free with accountability mechanisms to ensure that they do—namely, periodic drug testing. Although drug testing student athletes has been controversial ever since the Supreme Court upheld the practice in 1995 in *Vernonia School District 47J v. Acton*, a report released by the Department of Education in 2010 notes that schools with the policy had lower rates of drug use than schools that lacked the practice, though the effects are limited.[49]

After the death of seventeen-year-old Hunter Burkey in 2015, his school, Belpre High School, and the surrounding Ohio school district rolled out a policy of randomly drug testing student athletes and those participating in extracurricular activities. Those who failed their screens would be directed to counseling programs and faced a sliding scale of sanctions for future participation in athletic or extracurricular events from a temporary suspension to an outright ban.[50] Other schools, like Crivitz High School in Marinette County, Wisconsin, have adopted similar practices while also partnering with their local hospital to help cover the costs of testing.[51] Given that these programs are relatively new, there is not yet data regarding their effectiveness.

## CONCLUSION

On September 14, 2017, West Virginia governor Jim Justice announced
that he was stepping down as head coach of the boys' basketball team at
Greenbrier East High School.[52] The state's legislative session was scheduled
to begin just partway through the high school basketball season, and with a
heavy legislative agenda ahead—sure to be dominated in part by the opioid
crisis—the governor, like so many others, could no longer find the time.

Presented here is an account of the modest literature on rural schools,
teens, and the opioid crisis. By their very nature, the large-bore studies and
surveys that animate much of this chapter obscure the textured lives of the
afflicted: the students, the teachers, the sports coaches, the parents, and their
communities. Those lives, individual and collective, contain the separate-
yet-interconnected stories of how this problem began and how repair can
commence: at the level of each unique community, aided by—one is com-
pelled to add—serious funding from the federal government. While a reso-
lution to the crisis is still years away, with persistent and dedicated efforts,
the next upset in Logan, West Virginia, might just be the county's Wildcats
finally reclaiming the State's AA Title.

## NOTES

1  Mark Martin, "Ten Years Ago: Runnin Red Devils of 2006 Brought Title
   to Ravenswood," *Jackson Newspapers*, March 15, 2016, http://www.
   jacksonnewspapers.com/sports/20160314/ten-years-ago-runnin-red-
   devils-of-2006-brought-title-to-ravenswood.
2  "Keyser vs Ravenswood," MaxPreps.com, March 15, 2006, http://www.
   maxpreps.com/games/basketball-winter-05-06/keyser-vs-ravenswood/
   3-15-2006-DoLa1rl5kE-LSbe4VjVAnA.htm.
3  "Mt. View vs Logan," MaxPreps.com, March 15, 2006, http://www.
   maxpreps.com/games/basketball-winter-05-06/logan-vs-mt-view/3-15-2006-
   bvrTKG8qDE27OC_nK2rLag.htm#tab=recap&schoolid=.
4  Note: Baltimore is an independent city and not located within any county but
   is treated as a county for statistical purposes by the CDC; see: "CDC Wonder,"
   U.S. Department of Health and Human Services, Centers for Disease Control,
   accessed November 29, 2017, http://wonder.cdc.gov.
5  Note: Baltimore's overdose rate that year was 32.5 per 100,000. Logan County,
   West Virginia, was 65.9; see: "CDC Wonder."
6  Alyssa Rae, "Basketball Town to Ghost Town: The Story of Northfork,"
   *Fox 59*, December 5, 2014, http://www.wearewvproud.com/story/27560434/
   basketball-town-to-ghost-town-the-story-of-northfork.
7  Pamela Riney-Kehrberg, *The Routledge History of Rural America* (Abingdon:
   Taylor and Francis, 2016).

8  Kara Duffy, "Opioid Crisis: Putting a Life-Saving Drug in Schools," *CBS12. com*, July 11, 2017, http://cbs12.com/news/local/opioid-crisis-putting-a-life-saving-drug-in-schools.

9  "CDC Wonder."

10 Nora D. Volkow and A. Thomas Mclellan, "Opioid Abuse in Chronic Pain— Misconceptions and Mitigation Strategies," *New England Journal of Medicine* 374, no. 13 (March 2016), 1253–63.

11 National Institute on Drug Abuse, "Prescription and Over-the-Counter Medications," U.S. Department of Health and Human Services, National Institutes of Health, National Institute on Drug Abuse, November 24, 2015, https://www. drugabuse.gov/publications/drugfacts/prescription-over-counter-medications.

12 Anne Case and Sir Angus Deaton, "Mortality and Morbidity in the 21st Century," in *Brookings Papers on Economic Activity* (Washington, DC: Brookings Institution, 2017), https://www.brookings.edu/wp-content/uploads/2017/08/casetextsp17bpea.pdf.

13 "West Virginia Center for Children's Justice," West Virginia Center for Children's Justice, accessed November 29, 2017, http://www.handlewithcarewv.org/.

14 U.S. Department of Health and Human Services, Substance Abuse and Mental Health Services Administration, Office of Applied Studies, *The NSDUH Report: Children Living with Substance-Dependent or Substance-Abusing Parents: 2002 to 2007*, April 19, 2009, https://ok.gov/odmhsas/documents/ Children%20Living%20with%20Substance%20Dependent%20or%20 Abusing%20Parents%202002-2007.pdf.

15 Child Welfare Information Gateway, *Parental Substance Use and the Child Welfare System*, U.S. Department of Health and Human Services, Children's Bureau, October 2014, https://www.childwelfare.gov/pubPDFs/parentalsubabuse.pdf; and Jessica M. Solis et al., "Understanding the Diverse Needs of Children Whose Parents Abuse Substances," *Current Drug Abuse Reviews* 5, no. 2 (June 2012), 135–47.

16 Ibid.

17 Kristen Mascia, "I'm a 20-Year-Old Orphan Because of My Mom's Heroin Addiction," *Cosmopolitan*, December 1, 2016, http://www.cosmopolitan.com/ politics/a8349038/heroin-addiction-pain-killers-orphan/.

18 Kimber Paschall Richter and Gabriele Bammer, "A Hierarchy of Strategies Heroin-Using Mothers Employ to Reduce Harm to Their Children," *Journal of Substance Abuse Treatment* 19, no. 4 (December 2000), 403–13.

19 Amy B. Wang, "This Photo of an Officer Comforting a Baby Went Viral But There's More to the Story," *Washington Post*, September 6, 2016, https:// www.washingtonpost.com/news/inspired-life/wp/2016/09/03/touching-photo-shows-police-officer-comforting-baby-whose-parents-overdosed/?utm_term=. ad5f67855afd.

20 Diana Kronstadt, "Complex Developmental Issues of Prenatal Drug Exposure," *The Future of Children* 1, no. 1 (Spring 1991), 36–49, https://pdfs. semanticscholar.org/0e7f/fad78e01fe264ec9f0146f3323f2254effae.pdf.

21 U.S. Department of Health and Human Services, "The AFCARS Report," no. 24 (October 2017), https://www.acf.hhs.gov/sites/default/files/cb/afcarsreport24.pdf.

22  Wafaa Ahmed, Jeeihn Lee, and Hailey Valerio, *Supporting Vermont's Foster Parents through Innovative Systems of Support*, Nelson A. Rockefeller Center at Dartmouth College, Policy Research Shop, March 12, 2017, http://rockefeller. dartmouth.edu/sites/rockefeller.drupalmulti-prod.dartmouth.edu/files/prs_foster_ care_report_1617-03_final.pdf.

23  Rosa Rendon, "10 Percent of Grandparents Live with a Grandchild, Census Bureau Reports," U.S. Department of Commerce, U.S. Census Bureau, October 22, 2014, https://www.census.gov/newsroom/press-releases/2014/cb14-194. html.

24  Nina Williams-Mbengue and Kyle Ramirez, "Educational and Medical Consent Laws," National Conference of State Legislatures, February 17, 2017, http:// www.ncsl.org/research/human-services/educational-and-medical-consent-laws. aspx.

25  Perry Stein and Lindsey Bever, "The Opioid Crisis Is Straining the Nation's Foster-Care Systems," *Washington Post*, July 1, 2017, https://www. washingtonpost.com/national/the-opioid-crisis-is-straining-the-nations- foster-care-systems/2017/06/30/97759fb2-52a1–11e7–91eb-9611861a988f_ story.html?utm_term=.8c84ec7b3cd1.

26  Angela Sausser, Testimony on Sub. H.B. 49, before the Ohio Senate Health and Medicaid Subcommittee, 132nd Ohio General Assembly, 2017, http:// advocatesforohio.org/perch/resources/PCSAO-Subcommittee-Testimony.pdf.

27  Gary Tennis, "Fighting the Opioid Epidemic in the 2016–17 Budget," *Pennsylvania Governor Blog*, February 16, 2016, https://www.governor.pa.gov/blog-fighting- the-opioid-epidemic-in-the-2016-17-budget/; and Paula Seligson and Tim Reid, "Unbudgeted: How the Opioid Crisis Is Blowing a Hole in Small-Town America's Finances," *Reuters*, September 27, 2017, https://www.reuters.com/article/us-usa- opioids-budgets/unbudgeted-how-the-opioid-crisis-is-blowing-a-hole-in-small- town-americas-finances-idUSKCN1BU2LP.

28  Lisa Stark, "This West Virginia School Is Caring for Students, When Addicted Parents Can't," *PBS News Hour*, December 27, 2016, http://www.pbs.org/ newshour/bb/west-virginia-school-caring-students-addicted-parents-cant/.

29  "Mourners Bid Farewell," *Parkersburg News and Sentinel*, August 10, 2015, http://www.newsandsentinel.com/news/local-news/2015/08/mourners-bid- farewell-to-belpre-teenager-at-candlelight-vigil.

30  Richard A. Miech, Lloyd D. Johnston, Patrick M. O'Malley, Jerald G. Bachman, John E. Schulenberg, and Megan E. Patrick, *Monitoring the Future National Survey Results on Drug Use, 1975–2016: Volume I: Secondary School Students*, Institute for Social Research, University of Michigan, June 2017, http://www. monitoringthefuture.org//pubs/monographs/mtf-vol1_2016.pdf.

31  Ibid.

32  "CDC Wonder."

33  Shannon M. Monnat and Khary K. Rigg, "Examining Rural/Urban Differences in Prescription Opioid Misuse among US Adolescents," *Journal of Rural Health* 32, no. 2 (Spring 2016), 204–18; and April M. Young et al., "A Comparison of Rural and Urban Nonmedical Prescription Opioid Users' Lifetime and Recent Drug

Use," *American Journal of Drug and Alcohol Abuse* 38, no. 3 (May 2012), 220–27.

34 Young et al., "A Comparison"; and Rohit Shenoi, "Prescription Opioids in Children towards a Safer and Pain-Free Tomorrow," American Academy of Pediatrics, 1997, https://www.fda.gov/downloads/AdvisoryCommittees/CommitteesMeetingMaterials/Drugs/AnestheticAndAnalgesicDrugProductsAdvisoryCommittee/UCM522745.pdf.

35 Monnat and Rigg, "Examining Rural/Urban Differences"; and Young et al., "A Comparison."

36 Katherine M. Keyes et al., "Understanding the Rural-Urban Differences in Nonmedical Prescription Opioid Use and Abuse in the United States," *American Journal of Public Health* 104, no. 2 (February 2014), e52–e59.

37 Sam Quinones, *Dreamland: The True Tale of America's Opiate Epidemic* (New York: Bloomsbury, 2015), 212.

38 Jason A. Ford, "Nonmedical Prescription Drug Use among Adolescents: The Influence of Bonds to Family and School," *Youth & Society* 40, no. 3 (April 2009), 336–52.

39 Maryland State Department of Education, *Heroin and Opioid Awareness & Prevention Toolkit*, 2017, http://www.marylandpublicschools.org/Documents/heroinprevention/HeroinToolkit.pdf.

40 Philip T. Veliz, Carol Boyd, and Sean E. McCabe, "Nonmedical Prescription Opioid and Heroin Use among Adolescents Who Engage in Sports and Exercise," *Pediatrics* 138, no. 2 (August 2016), 1–11, http://pediatrics.aappublications.org/content/138/2/e20160677; and Associated Press, "Beyond 'Just Say No': Schools Teach about Opioid Dangers," *STAT*, January 27, 2017, https://www.statnews.com/2017/01/27/opioid-dangers-schools-students/.

41 Meg Holmberg, "Engaging Schools in the Juvenile Drug Court: Promising Strategies from the Field," National Council of Juvenile and Family Court Judges, 2013, http://www.ncjfcj.org/sites/default/files/Engaging%20School_Strategies%20in%20the%20Field%20%281%29.pdf.

42 D. Paul Moberg and Andrew J. Finch, "Recovery High Schools: A Descriptive Study of School Programs and Students," *Journal of Groups in Addiction & Recovery* 2 (2008), 128–61, https://www.ncbi.nlm.nih.gov/pmc/articles/PMC2629137/.

43 Trevor Shirley, "Sec. of Education Betsey DeVos Visits Indianapolis Charter School," *Fox 59*, September 15, 2017, http://fox59.com/2017/09/15/sec-of-education-betsy-devos-visits-indianapolis-charter-school/.

44 Tricia Harte, "Graduating Hope: A Look at Indiana's Only High School for Addicted Teens," *Fox 59*, June 2, 2017, http://fox59.com/2017/06/02/graduating-hope-a-look-at-indianas-only-high-school-for-addicted-teens/.

45 Association of Recovery Schools, "Find a School," accessed November 29, 2017, https://recoveryschools.org/find-a-school/.

46 Philip T. Veliz, Carol Boyd, and Sean E. McCabe, "Playing Through Pain: Sports Participation and Nonmedical Use of Opioid Medications among Adolescents," *American Journal of Public Health* 103, no. 5 (2013), e28–e30.

47  Veliz, Boyd, and McCabe, "Nonmedical Prescription Opioid and Heroin Use."

48  Philip T. Veliz, Carol Boyd, and Sean E. McCabe, "Nonmedical Use of Pre-scription Opioids and Heroin Use among Adolescents Involved in Competitive Sports," *Journal of Adolescent Health* 60, no. 3 (March 2017), 346–49, https://www.clinicalkey.com/#!/content/playContent/1-s2.0-S1054139X16303706?retur nurl=null&referrer=null.

49  *Vernonia School District 47J v. Acton*, 515 U.S. 646 (1995), https://www.law. cornell.edu/supct/html/94-590.ZO.html; and James-Burdumy, Brian Goesling, John Deke, Eric Einspruch, and Marsha Silverberg, *The Effectiveness of Mandatory-Random Student Drug Testing*, U.S. Department of Education, Institute of Education Sciences, July 2010, https://ies.ed.gov/ncee/pubs/20104025/ pdf/20104025.pdf.

50  Aaron Payne, "Opioid High: Students Face a Different Kind of Test," *West Virginia Public Broadcasting*, September 9, 2016, http://wvpublic.org/post/ opioid-high-students-face-different-kind-test#stream/0.

51  Cole Higgins, "Crivitz High School to Subject Some Students to Random Drug Testing," WeAreGreenbay.com, August 17, 2015, http://www.wearegreenbay. com/news/local-news/crivitz-high-school-to-subject-some-students-to-random-drug-testing/207895501.

52  Brad Mcelhinny, "Gov. Justice Relinquishing Half His Coaching Duties at Greenbrier East," *WV Metro News*, September 14, 2017, http://wvmetronews. com/2017/09/14/governor-justice-says-hes-retired-from-coaching-one-of-his-teams/.

*Chapter 4*

# The Power of Place: Rural Identity and the Politics of Rural School Reform

Sara Dahill-Brown and Ashley Jochim

In many regards, rural districts look much the same as urban ones: school boards are democratically elected; superintendents lead and oversee daily operations; and teachers, parents, and taxpayers negotiate over resources and programs. And just as reforms to urban school systems live and die on the back of politics, so do rural ones. But how do the political realities, that rural districts face, differ from their peers in big cities? This chapter will consider the basic organizing principles for education politics in rural districts and the dynamics of the actors, interest groups, and coalitions that shape what rural districts are able to accomplish.

Over the past two decades, school reform politics has been shaped by teachers' unions and the decisions of state and federal policymakers, as well as general government actors like mayors. This chapter seeks to show why these actors are less well-positioned to support rural school reform, given the absence of well-organized interest groups, lack of local political leadership, and the positioning of rural identity in opposition to reform strategies developed by urban elites and state and federal policymakers. Thus, while rural schools face deep challenges, the politics of rural communities place strict limits on the extent to which outsiders can lend their ideas and support.

This chapter begins by describing the challenges facing rural school districts, which at once parallel and diverge from those confronting urban districts. Then, the role of outsiders—urban elites as well as state and federal leaders—in driving the politics of reform in rural areas is described. This analysis suggests that rural identity often underlies resistance to these efforts, but can also shape local conflict and cooperation among traditional actors in educational politics: local school boards, teachers' unions, parent groups, and local businesses. Understanding and navigating this tension between rural insiders and urban outsiders is a key to supporting rural schools.

# FRAMING THE CHALLENGES OF RURAL
# SCHOOL REFORM

Despite the fact that rural districts comprised 53 percent of all school districts during the 2013–2014 school year and enrolled 18 percent of all K–12 public school students in the country, including about 20 percent of all students in poverty,[1] rural schools are typically an afterthought in discussions of education reform. The guiding school-reform fights over the past three decades—for example, mayoral control, state takeovers, and school choice—often leave rural districts untouched.

At first glance, the focus on urban schools to the exclusion of rural ones might appear driven by the relative academic success of students in rural areas. According to the National Assessment of Educational Progress (NAEP), rural students outperformed their urban peers and near to levels of children in suburban schools at grades four, eight, and twelve in reading, science, and math.[2] Likewise, rural students graduate from high school at rates substantially higher than students in cities—80.6 percent in 2009–2010 compared with 71.1 percent—and very near to the rate attained by students in the suburbs, 81.4 percent.[3]

However, rural schools face a number of significant challenges. Young adults in rural areas are among the least likely to be enrolled in any postsecondary program.[4] Gaps in achievement and attainment between female and male students are also growing as rates of postsecondary enrollment for young women in rural areas exceeding those for young men.[5]

And, like urban schools, rural schools struggle to address persistent educational inequalities that divide low-income families from more affluent ones, and white children from Latino and African-American children.[6] Rural communities have undergone substantial demographic and economic changes, including rising poverty and growing ethnic diversity, which make these changes all the more salient for understanding the challenges facing rural schools.[7]

While cities often tap cultural and economic capital to address challenges in the schools, rural communities are less able to draw upon these resources. Rural communities have long possessed fewer employment opportunities, lower levels of educational attainment, and higher poverty rates.[8] Indeed, the Economic Research Service found that 85 percent of all "persistent-poverty" counties were rural—accounting for 15.2 percent of all rural counties.[9] These trends were exacerbated by the Great Recession, and rural communities were less likely to recover compared to either their suburban or urban peers.[10]

Rural communities also face rising health challenges—what Anne Case and Angus Deaton called "deaths of despair"—spurring from drug overdoses, alcohol poisonings, and suicides.[11] As Janet Adamy and Paul Overberg put it in the *Wall Street Journal*, "In terms of poverty, college attainment, teenage births, divorce, deaths from heart disease and cancer, reliance on federal disability insurance, and male labor-force participation, rural counties now rank the worst."[12]

These compounding challenges have helped to accelerate "brain drain" in rural communities. While the educational attainment of people living in rural communities has increased over time, fewer than one in five adults in rural areas possess a bachelor's degree or more.[13] Out-migration from rural areas and small towns to suburban areas and cities is a century-old trend, but the decline of rural America's economic base has made it even more difficult for young people to stay in the communities in which they were raised, and two-thirds of rural communities lost population between 2010 and 2014.[14]

This makes investment in rural education all the more challenging because, as Stephan Goetz put it, "rural areas face the prospect of educating adolescents only to see the better trained ones move away, with the owners of fixed resources incurring most of the local tax burden."[15]

These trends place increased pressure on rural schools to perform. Like urban schools, rural schools are expected to mitigate gaps in educational achievement and attainment, enable rural students to succeed in college and careers, and simultaneously serve as lead partners in community revitalization efforts. Yet, because of the status of the rural economy, succeeding in these endeavors may very well spur more out-migration, as rural students seek opportunities in the cities. As Eleanor Krause and Richard V. Reeves find, rural counties characterized by more outward migration were *more* likely to support intergenerational upward mobility.[16]

## "OUTSIDERS" AND RURAL IDENTITY IN SCHOOL REFORM

In the twentieth and twenty-first centuries, political leaders and education reformers who primarily operated beyond rural communities have vacillated between ignoring the needs of rural areas and problematizing them as backwards, in need of modernization. Educational improvement in rural schools is, therefore, frequently neglected—just seventy-one of the education-related bills enacted by state legislatures between 2001 and 2016 mentioned rural communities at all.[17] Yet, when rural educational improvement has risen on public agendas, the terms of debate have often been established by urban actors who sought to impose their vision of a good education on rural communities.

Consider the Progressives, widely acknowledged as having transformed educational systems and pedagogical practices throughout the United States

during a period of rapid urbanization. While historians have written extensively about the Progressive movement's impacts on education in cities like
Chicago and New York, Progressive reformers in the early twentieth century
also targeted rural areas.

They believed that many urban problems—as well as the larger social,
political, economic, and moral decline of America—were rooted in the decay
of rural communities, and they distrusted the capacity of rural farmers and
laborers to supervise their own school systems.[18] In Tennessee and Iowa,
Progressives worked to revitalize physical infrastructure, consolidate schools
and districts, and institute home-economics programs, all in the name of
progress.[19]

However, in both Tennessee and Iowa—as well as other places around
the country—rural people resented and resisted these efforts. In Tennessee,
reformers failed to engage with the extraordinary salience of racial stratification and the exploitative practices of farm tenancy. In Iowa, vigorous opposition successfully stymied many consolidation efforts.

Reformers often failed to appreciate the connection between economies,
place, and culture; they primarily hailed from industrialized urban centers
and sought to impose the logic of industrial communities on agriculturally
dependent and increasingly marginalized rural communities.[20] Local community identities and inequalities therefore mediated the impact of reform
efforts.

An often-unrecognized legacy of Progressive-era educational reforms has
been a sense among rural communities that education reforms are largely
initiated from the outside, with little concern for the particular needs of local
communities or for the uniquely prominent position of schools in their communities. This perception lingers and may contribute to feelings of resentment toward outsiders, as members of rural communities perceive local
traditions or ways of life disrespected or threatened.[21]

As Kathy Cramer reported in her seminal case study of politics in small
town and rural Wisconsin, "There are many people in rural areas who . . . have
strong resentment toward the cities and urban elites. They feel as though they
are not getting their fair share of power—no one is really listening to them."[22]

## Rural Resistance and Influence in Education Reform

An irony of these sentiments is that rural communities are, in fact, powerful
sites of resistance to federal and state education-reform efforts. Throughout
the twentieth century, rural communities have flexed their political muscles
to slow, weaken, or reverse a number of significant reforms, including consolidation, desegregation, statewide curricula and standards, and teacher collective bargaining.[23]

Each of these policy efforts was spearheaded by outsiders, and rural opponents believed that they threatened local, community control, represented positions not reflective of rural values, or were associated with unfavorable partisans. Bills favored by urban delegations are less likely to pass through state legislatures than those affecting rural areas and small towns.[24]

Rural communities possess the political clout to resist reform efforts in part because they enjoy a substantial representational advantage in Congress. In 2016, just 17 percent of the population could have theoretically elected a majority in the Senate.[25]

This representational advantage is also present at the state level. Up until the 1960s, just 35 percent of American voters elected as many 50 percent of state legislators due to state-redistricting decisions that favored rural communities in times of growing urban populations.[26] Even as rural legislative clout has been diminished, rural communities have benefited from partisan allegiances that enable them to build winning coalitions with nonrural communities (largely through the Republican Party). As Alan Greenblatt wrote in *Governing*, rural state delegations "are still able to hit well above their weight in numerous states."[27]

Rural influence can go beyond obstructionism, of course. Rural education leaders have won reforms to state and federal education policy. They have played leading roles in school-finance equalization and adequacy cases around the country, including serving as plaintiffs in cases stemming from Colorado, Pennsylvania, Mississippi, New Jersey, and South Carolina and regularly voice opposition to rules advanced by state education agencies. As leaders of the opposition in the move to unionize teachers in the 1960s, rural communities also helped to advance controversial reforms to collective bargaining in Wisconsin that curtailed the influence of unions on rural schools.[28]

In sum, rural communities are major players in education reform, driving a "hidden politics." Their stories are less central to the debates that dominate federal and state governments, and their plights are too often ignored by education-reform advocacy groups and policymakers.

And yet, their influence on education is substantial, leveraging the power of representational advantages and durable coalitions between rural and nonrural Republicans to function as incredibly effective veto players, able to slow down or halt new reform efforts, even as they are less-often able to set the reform agenda. As the *New York Times* "Upshot" put it, "Rural America, even as it laments its economic weakness, retains vastly disproportionate [political] strength."[29]

## Rural Identity as a Defining Feature of Rural Education Politics

The tension between insiders and outsiders animates more than just reactions to state and federal policy reforms; it is also a central axis of conflict around which local educational politics revolve. Even local actors perceived to be on the wrong side of a debate can be framed rhetorically—and dismissed, silenced, or delegitimized—by painting them as outsiders. In part, the power of this narrative in rural-education politics is a result of the particular characteristics and high salience of place-based social identities in rural areas. These local identities share common markers, in that the same social, political, and economic forces buffet rural communities across the country.

Differences between rural and urban economies help to animate insider–outsider dynamics in rural communities. Rural adults are more likely to report working blue-collar jobs as compared to their urban peers. Likewise, rural residents are more likely to identify as members of the lower and working classes as opposed to the middle and upper classes. That sense of belonging to the lower and working classes appears to have strengthened over time: in 1996, almost 60 percent of rural residents identified as members of the lower or working classes; by 2016, that proportion had risen to 70 percent.[30]

As rural and urban places have followed distinctive paths, rural communities increasingly report disconnection from, and resentment of, cities and urban elites. In 2017, only 29 percent of rural respondents agreed that people in cities shared similar values to their own. Notably, the sense of separateness is asymmetrical: city dwellers were much more likely to see similarities between themselves and rural people, with almost 49 percent agreeing that people in rural areas and small towns shared their values.[31]

More than just disconnection, however, people in rural areas express a sense that they have been passed over and disrespected, especially by news media and political leaders who pay more attention and direct greater resources toward urban centers. On one recent survey, more than half of rural respondents reported that they believed the government does more to help big cities.[32] People in rural communities are also more likely than suburban and urban residents to express deep distrust of government institutions, holding them at least partly accountable for the hardships of recent decades.[33]

At the same time, there is a pervasive sense of shared values and pride that binds rural communities together. The same surveys that reveal a divide between rural and urban peoples also provide evidence that, within rural communities, there is a strong cohesiveness. When asked if they believed that people in other rural areas and small towns shared values similar to their own, 74 percent of those living in rural areas agreed. By comparison, just 57 percent of respondents living in cities felt their values were shared by other urban residents.[34]

A strong rural identity is also facilitated by the fact that rural populations tend to share other politically salient identity categories, including race and ethnicity, age, religiosity, partisanship, and political ideology. A substantial majority of the people in rural areas identify as white—though, as discussed later in this chapter, this is both unevenly true and in flux. Rural residents are older on average: nearly a quarter are over the age of sixty-five versus 21 percent in suburban locales and 18 percent in cities.[35] People in rural places are also more likely to identify as Christians (81 percent).[36]

Conservative political ideologies and Republican Party identification are particularly dominant in rural places. In a time of extreme discord between liberals and conservatives, Democrats and Republicans, these allegiances likely play a key role, both in shaping a sense of belonging within rural communities and perpetuating distrust of urban communities. More rural residents identify as conservative compared with those in suburban and urban areas, and they vote accordingly. Throughout the spring of 2017, rural communities maintained the highest rates of approval for President Trump.[37]

School districts distributed across rural and urban environments are therefore embedded in vastly different partisan political climates, with those differences often reinforced by these other, overlapping identities. During the 2012–2013 school year, 75 percent of school districts that were classified as serving a rural area were located in counties where the Republican presidential candidate, Mitt Romney, earned more votes than the incumbent, Barack Obama. By comparison, just 41 percent of school districts classified as serving a city in that year were located in counties where Mitt Romney earned more votes than Barack Obama.[38]

The more distant or remote a school district's location, the more Republican its voters are likely to be. For example, 65 percent of "fringe rural" school districts (near to urban areas) were in counties that supported the 2012 Republican candidate for president, compared with 76 percent of "distant rural" (farther from urban areas) school districts and 81 percent of "remote rural" school districts.

Results from the 2016 presidential election, matched to school-district data from the 2014–2015 school year (the most recent Local Education Agency Universe Survey available), suggest that the partisan environment in which rural school districts are embedded may be growing more strongly Republican, and therefore more distinct from the political context in city districts. For instance, 91 percent of remote-rural districts were located in counties where the Republican candidate, Donald Trump, won more votes than the Democratic candidate, Hillary Clinton, compared with 81 percent in the previous presidential contest.[39]

For rural communities with specific sets of shared values and closely held social identities defined partly in opposition to big cities, parents and local stakeholders understandably want schools to reflect and validate their values. Schools that fail to adopt culturally responsive pedagogy and curricula will risk alienating students as they strive to prepare children—not for the communities and economies in which they grow up, but instead for more urban communities to which they might migrate one day.

At the same time, parents, teachers, and rural community leaders recognize that children will often leave the communities in which they are raised. Nearly 60 percent of rural people surveyed in 2017 said that they would tell their children to leave in search of better economic opportunities when they came of age. Rural education reform must acknowledge and negotiate the tension between preparing children to be successful in the wider world and affirming the communities in which they are growing up.

## POLITICAL CONSTRAINTS ON RURAL SCHOOL REFORM

If rural identity is shaped in part vis-à-vis rural communities' opposition to reforms advanced from urban elites and state and federal policymakers, then rural school reform hinges on coalition building at the local level. Much has been written about the prospects and challenges of assembling broad-based coalitions in support of urban school-reform agendas. This work highlights the importance of "governing coalitions"—unified by a shared understanding of the problems in urban schools, reform priorities, and a system for allocating political power among the many organized interests that dominate cities.[40] These offer the stability necessary for advancing education improvement initiatives.

Marshaling politics to support educational improvement is never an easy task. Interest groups vie for power and influence, political leaders seek to make their mark, and community members can organize to fight even the most well-intentioned reforms. While rural school districts share many characteristics with their more urban peers, their politics can be especially constraining when it comes to advancing school reform.

### Rural School Boards: More Alike Than Different

At first glance, rural school systems share many of the same features as urban ones. Rural school boards, like the vast majority of suburban and urban school boards, are elected. Few rural boards have faced the threat of state takeover, which more frequently target large urban districts characterized by patterns of financial insolvency, corruption, and low academic achievement.

While urban school boards are often depicted as dysfunctional, with high levels of conflict among board members and between boards and the superintendent, rural boards are more similar than different from their peers in nonrural school districts.

Unsurprisingly, given the partisan context in which they are embedded, rural school boards are less likely to host liberal board members and more likely to host conservative ones. However, a plurality of board members in both types of settings identifies as moderate or nonpartisan, likely reflecting long-standing norms around insulating local school districts from traditional partisan politics.

Conventional wisdom suggests that rural boards are characterized by lower levels of conflict compared to their peers in nonrural settings, due to the close-knit communities that characterize small-town life. But we find no evidence that rural districts are much different than their nonrural peers. Board members in both types of settings were not likely to report high levels of conflict or personal disagreements among them or that conflicts often resurfaced over time. Both types of board members were only moderately more likely to agree that school-board coalitions tended to form along predictable lines.

Indeed, the most significant distinguishing feature between rural and nonrural school boards is the fact that rural board members are much more likely to run for their seat unopposed. This feature could offer rural boards some advantages over their nonrural peers, given that high levels of board turnover can disrupt initiatives that aim to improve schools and increase the likelihood of conflict between the board and superintendent.

## Fewer Interest Group Groups, Fewer Opportunities to Develop Reform Coalitions

At first glance, rural places may seem well-positioned to escape the political conflicts that emerge between interest groups in big cities. While little data exist on the geography of interest-group politics, the neglect of rural communities in the interest-group literature offers suggestive evidence that rural places are not the primary sites of interest-group organization. Rural communities, by virtue of their lower population densities, weaker economic base, and historically limited demographic diversity, are likely to face few of the same interest-group pressures that big, city school systems do.

But district superintendents and school-board members in rural communities do have to confront one of the most formidable forces in education politics: teachers' unions. While many rural districts have a collective-bargaining agreement, evidence suggests that rural teachers' unions are less powerful than their peers in big cities. Teachers working in rural districts have the lowest teacher salaries; are less likely to be offered health, dental, or life insurance benefits; and access fewer pay incentives (e.g., National Board certifications).[41]

As Campbell Scribner describes, rural communities "cast statewide teachers' unions as the instigators and primary beneficiaries of rural school consolidation," thereby solidifying the position of small-town America as the primary opponent of the organizing efforts of teachers' unions, with long-term consequences for public sector labor law.[42]

The weakness of teachers' unions in rural communities may seem like a boon for reform-minded superintendents and school boards, as many advocates for change in America's K–12 system attribute the failure to realize their goals largely to unions. But this perspective misses the fact that a weak opposition is neither necessary nor sufficient for ambitious new initiatives to be seeded and take root.

And, perhaps more problematically, rural communities face their own set of entrenched business interests, which can limit prospects for new programs to gain the requisite political support. Rural communities tend to reflect specialized economies, typically relying heavily upon the agriculture, manufacturing, or energy industries. According to the Economic Research Service, 70 percent of rural counties in the United States are considered "dependent" on particular industries.[43]

Industry concentration creates two types of challenges for rural education. One relates to the need for skilled labor—to the extent that the main source of employment in rural communities relies upon labor that does not require a college degree; the business community may not be a strong source of support for initiatives that seek to prepare students for post-K–12 educational opportunities.

The second relates to a foundational challenge in rural communities: the lack of financial resources to support new initiatives. To the extent that rural communities rely upon property taxes to fund schools, the concentration of particular industries, like agriculture, which often qualify for special tax exemptions and rely upon large and valuable tracts of property, limits opportunities to make investments in rural schools. In a number of cases, including Midwestern states like Minnesota and Ohio, statewide conflicts over funding for schools often pit rural communities—as represented by agricultural interests—against urban communities, which seek to raise taxes to support additional funding for schools.[44]

## Racial Politics Presents Both Risks and Opportunities for Rural Schools

Race has long acted as a potent political force in rural communities, as it has in urban ones. But whereas in cities, racial and ethnic minorities have gained political influence through efforts to organize historically disenfranchised communities and secure positions of power in city government, rural ethnic minorities historically have been less well-positioned to seed effective political coalitions in support of rural schools.

Rural America is frequently assumed to be home to few ethnic minorities. This, of course, has never been true. But, unlike cities, where America's vision of an ethnic "melting pot" was borne, ethnic minorities in rural communities tend to be fragmented.[45]

As Daniel Lichter explains, "America's rural ethnic minorities are often geographically and socially isolated from mainstream America and easily forgotten or ignored. They live on Indian reservations, in southern rural areas and small towns in the so called black belt, and in the Colonias along the lower Rio Grande Valley."[46] Compared to their peers living in cities, rural minorities are much more likely to be poor.[47]

To date, rural schools have struggled to incorporate ethnic minorities, especially immigrants. Rural schools typically lack specialists who can support Latino immigrants' language needs and may lack strategies for engaging families whose immigration, language, and educational status all pose barriers to stronger engagement (and representation) in local school systems. Rural white families are significantly more likely than rural African-American and Latino families to rate their local schools as "excellent" or "good."[48]

While the challenges presented to rural schools through immigration are relatively new, rural schools have long faced difficulties addressing gaps in educational opportunity for rural African Americans, the vast majority of which live in the South. As of 1990—more than three decades after *Brown v. Board of Education*—rural blacks had the lowest educational attainment: lower than urban blacks and both rural and urban whites.[49]

In theory, *Brown* sought to improve the educational prospects of blacks in the segregated South. But, ironically, the most immediate effect of the decision was the loss of black educators—with 38,000 African Americans losing their jobs as teachers and administrators between 1954 and 1965.[50]

But rural communities have faced unprecedented demographic changes that have the potential to shift the political dynamic around rural school reform. Between 1980 and 2009, rural ethnic diversity increased by nearly 40 percent; in the past decade, diversity has increased more rapidly in rural counties than anywhere else.[51] A UCLA study of racial and ethnic segregation in schools identified rural systems as the locations where integration was, on average, moving forward, compared with suburban and urban schools, where integration has stalled or reversed.[52]

These shifts—driven in large part by patterns of Latino immigration associated with business investments in rural communities—have reinvigorated debates over immigration and community, even as they have brought new life into "dying" towns with declining populations.[53] These conversations have potential to shift the politics of rural education in significant ways, since Latino immigrants are younger and more likely to have children, compared to white residents in rural communities.

## State and Federal Reforms: More Hindrance Than Help

Rural schools have not been central to the policy-reform efforts launched by states and the federal government in recent years. But that does not mean leaders in rural communities cannot leverage this work to benefit their own schools. As Paul Manna discusses, policy entrepreneurs in a federal system often use the justifications and capabilities of other levels of government in order to advance an initiative.[54] Thus, we observe state and district superintendents hitching their coattails to ambitious reform priorities launched from elsewhere.

But rural districts are rarely well-poised to capitalize on these efforts. Rural communities often express distinctive reform priorities that challenge basic precepts of the ideas embraced by urban elites and Washington. Public-opinion data suggest that residents of rural communities and small towns are less likely to embrace either private schools or charter schools, the main types of school choice that states and the federal government have sought to support.[55] And when national reform leaders like former secretary of education Arne Duncan called on all schools—rural included—to launch ambitious turnaround plans that included firing teachers and principals, many rural school districts balked.[56]

Even when considering the lofty and seemingly uncontroversial ideas about what public schools should strive for, rural communities differ from their urban peers. Less than half of rural school superintendents believe that college attendance is an important measure of public-school effectiveness, compared to 61 percent of superintendents in city or suburban school districts.[57] Ideas like school choice, charter schools, teacher evaluation, and school closures may have a place in rural communities, as some argue, but they are too often divorced from the challenges that rural communities face, leaving local leaders to "go it alone" as they carve out their reform agendas.

## Rural Superintendents: Constraints and Opportunities for Influence

The urban superintendency has been described as an impossible job for good reason. Urban superintendents are expected to perform superhero functions: raise achievement for all, close achievement gaps, keep the peace with unions and other school employees, and respond to myriad other demands stemming from states and the federal government. They do not control their own agendas but instead are "whipsawed by the demands of competing power centers within the system."[58]

However, there is little question that the political environment that rural superintendents face is simpler than those that exist in big cities. Teachers' unions are less formidable, school-board members less ambitious, and interest groups mostly lack the strength or diversity that exists in urban areas. Yet, rural superintendents are more professionally isolated, and this presents a distinct challenge.

As one superintendent confessed in a study now almost three decades old, "You know, everybody always thinks the city districts are so difficult to manage. But when you're a superintendent in a small district and all by yourself, you have a lot of the same tasks. Not the numbers, of course, but the same tasks. . . . And you do it all by yourself."[59] Or to put it perhaps more poignantly, in the words of another superintendent from the same study, "I was working 15 to 17 hour days. . . . All I was doing was oil tanks and asbestos. In a larger district, you could delegate [that stuff]. In a small district, you do it all."

Leaders of rural districts are expected to perform the same superhero functions as their urban peers with far fewer staff, but also with more-limited community resources. Rural schools typically possess less funding, lower teacher and principal salaries and fewer benefits, more out-of-field teachers, and fewer specialists trained to address gaps in learning. Compared to urban and suburban districts, rural districts are less able to offer instructional and other kinds of support to struggling teachers and principals, due in large part to their weaker economies of scale. And rural communities struggle to support students' out-of-school health and social needs, given the weaknesses in county and municipal government.

Rural superintendents also have to wrestle with a unique dimension of rural politics. What may be lacking in terms of organized forms of political mobilization can be more than made up by personal conflicts with the friends and neighbors, many of whom will either work for the superintendent or send their children to schools in the district. While big-city superintendents routinely make changes to their staff—executed through depersonalized human-resources departments—rural superintendents regularly confront the fact that a demotion or termination can be undertaken at significant personal costs.

Rural superintendents who want to press for change quickly find out just how fraught such efforts can be. A recommendation to deny tenure to a struggling teacher, a proposal to implement a new curriculum, or a discovery of fraud in the business office can quickly foment discontent among the community and between the board and the superintendent. Because rural superintendents have fewer political allies to rely upon, these conflicts can result in boards overruling the superintendent or, worse yet, forcing the superintendent out.

And while urban superintendents also face organized political challenges, rural superintendents struggle because the communities of which they are a part are so tightly knit.[60] As one rural superintendent noted, "You have to know who's on your chess board, who the kings and queens are, and who the players are. . . . They're not always the people who have been elected or appointed to any position. It's the informal system [too]."[61]

One way the rural superintendents can expand their power despite these constraints is to leverage their position to influence policy developments in the state legislature and state education agency (SEA). In a number of states, rural school-district associations help to coordinate efforts to pressure the state legislature, the courts, and the SEA on new initiatives, and it is not uncommon for these efforts to find success.[62] Opposition from rural superintendents can also stymie progress on state reforms, including proposals to expand school choice and put in place new funding formulas.[63]

At the same time, many rural superintendents are not well-positioned to advance their causes in the statehouse. Superintendents of small rural districts confront limits on their capacity given tiny administrative staffs. Moreover, they face collective-action dilemmas in coordinating among hundreds of other small districts.

As "jacks and janes of all trades," superintendents of small rural districts are often overwhelmed with leading their districts, much less monitoring and lobbying state legislatures. Among states where rural districts are larger—due to countywide district boundaries—and the number of rural districts is small, the rural superintendent may be better able to press for reform in the state legislature or with the SEA.

When rural superintendents lack the connections, experiences, or capacity to influence state political processes directly, they must rely upon other avenues. Most salient for many rural superintendents is their state representative. But these can prove fickle allies in the work of school reform. State legislators may care about local schools, but they are also accountable to voters on other matters and face lobbying pressures from business interests and citizens who may resist the efforts of a reform-minded superintendent.

Perhaps unsurprisingly, many rural superintendents leave their jobs for greener pastures.[64] Jason Grissom and Stephanie Anderson find that superintendent turnover typically results in superintendents moving from smaller districts to larger ones and from rural districts to suburban ones, adding one more dimension to the "brain drain" that rural communities confront.[65]

## LOOKING FORWARD: ADVANCING SCHOOL REFORM THROUGH POLITICS

The conventional wisdom suggests that urban school systems are "ungovernable" due to the entrenched patterns of political conflict that dominate cities. As seen in the preceding pages, while rural schools do not face the same types of political challenges, politics very much informs what local, state, and federal policymakers can hope to accomplish in their efforts to improve rural education.

As in cities, politics serves as a constraint on rural school reform. The power of rural identity means that state and federal reform efforts must tread carefully in rural places—or be cast aside as yet another "outside" initiative to improve rural schools. While rural schools lack a few of the same kinds of interest groups that make big-city school districts so political, they too are shaped by the whims of organized interest groups and the personal convictions of vocal community members.

It is easy to read through the catalogue of challenges facing rural schools in light of these political constraints and lose hope in the prospects for meaningful improvement. But rural communities do possess advantages that are lacking in big cities and which may offer a path forward.

Schools are uniquely positioned in rural communities to serve as community anchors. The personal relationships and "smallness" that add challenges to a rural superintendent's job also enhance opportunities for problem-solving. In a time in which debates over education and other policy issues in state legislatures and Congress break down in the face of ideological polarization and contempt for those who voice dissention, personal connection just might be the *most* powerful strategy for negotiating conflicts and identifying shared values.

Rural schools also stand out in terms of the connections fostered between schools and the larger community. Parental involvement and support for local schools is generally higher in rural places than it is in cities. And rural schools are central players in community life, with schools sometimes offering the only dedicated space for community gathering—whether at a Friday night football game or a local theater performance.

Approaching the work of rural-school improvement through the lens of politics suggests that progress hinges on assembling a strong base of support. Doing this work in rural communities will look different than it does in urban ones—where powerful actors like mayors can intervene to unify fragmented interest groups. Rural superintendents have essential roles to play, as their position affords them prestige and opportunity for influence; but, as this account of their challenges reveals, superintendents cannot do this work alone.

States and the federal government also have crucial roles to play in supporting local-improvement initiatives. But to ensure these efforts help, rather than hinder, this support must recognize that rural communities derive much strength from the positioning of their identity in opposition to the inclinations of urban elites and state and federal policymakers.

Recognizing this requires a new conception of the role of state and federal policy in the work of rural schools—one grounded in *supporting* local initiative-taking, rather than suffocating it. As Jeffrey Henig and Clarence Stone observe, "The best [state and federal governments] can do is to tilt the pinball machine in a direction that makes positive outcomes more likely."

While this chapter has offered some ideas and evidence on the politics of rural education, it has not given sufficient treatment to the variability in the challenges and traditions that shape rural schools and community life more generally. Rural places can vary as much with one another as they do with big cities. This variability has important implications for understanding the particulars of politics in rural education: the problems, interests, and prospects for reform.

As this chapter cannot provide answers to all the questions regarding the politics of rural education, it can serve as a call for others to treat rural schools as serious subjects of inquiry. If rural education is an afterthought in the conversations of state and federal advocates working in education, it is a footnote for education researchers. But as has been shown, rural schools offer fresh opportunities to understand public education and its politics. Perhaps more importantly, they are likely to shape American education in the years to come.

## NOTES

1  U.S. Department of Education, National Center for Education Statistics, "Common Core of Data (CCD): Local Education Agency Universe Survey," accessed November 28, 2017, https://nces.ed.gov/ccd/pubagency.asp.

2  Stephen Provasnik, Angelina KewalRamani, Mary McLaughlin Coleman, Lauren Gilbertson, Will Herring, and Qingshu Xie, "Status of Education in Rural America," U.S. Department of Education, Institute of Education Sciences, National Center for Education Statistics, July 25, 2007, https://nces.ed.gov/pubs2007/2007040.pdf.

3  U.S. Department of Education, National Center for Education Statistics, "Common Core of Data (CCD): Local Education Agency Universe Survey Dropout and Completion Restricted-Use Data File, School Year 2009–10 (Version 2a)," 2011, https://nces.ed.gov/ccd/drpagency.asp.

4  Note: In 2015, young people in rural areas (ages eighteen to twenty-four) are less likely to be enrolled in any postsecondary program: 29.3 percent compared with 47.7 percent in cities, 42.3 percent in suburbs, and 41.2 percent in towns. See U.S. Department of Education, National Center for Education Statistics, "Table B.3.b.-1 Percentage of Persons Ages 18–29 Enrolled in Colleges or Universities, by Age Group, 4-Category Local, and Sex: 2015," 2015, https://nces.ed.gov/surveys/ruraled/tables/b.3.b.-1.asp.

5  Ibid.

6  Daniel Showalter, Robert Klein, Jerry Johnson, Sara L. Hartman, *Why Rural Matters 2015–2016*, The Rural School and Community Trust, June 2017, http://www.ruraledu.org/user_uploads/file/WRM-2015-16.pdf.

7  Gary Orfield and Erica Frankenberg, *The Last Have Become First: Rural and Small Town America Lead the Way on Desegregation*, The Civil Rights Project, UCLA, January 2008, http://escholarship.org/uc/item/5062t6qs; and U.S.

Department of Agriculture, "Racial and Ethnic Diversity Is Increasing in Rural America," 2016, https://www.ers.usda.gov/webdocs/publications/44331/10597_page7.pdf?v=41055.

8  U.S. Department of Agriculture, *Rural America at a Glance, 2015 Edition*, 2015, https://www.ers.usda.gov/webdocs/publications/44015/55581_eib145.pdf?v=42397.

9  U.S. Department of Agriculture, "Child Poverty," Economic Research Service, U.S. Department of Agriculture, accessed November 28, 2017, https://www.ers.usda.gov/topics/rural-economy-population/rural-poverty-well-being/child-poverty/.

10  Note: According to the ACS, rural poverty is estimated at 18.4 percent while urban poverty is estimated at 15.1 percent. See U.S. Department of Agriculture, *Rural America at a Glance, 2016 Edition*, 2016, https://www.ers.usda.gov/webdocs/publications/80894/eib-162.pdf?v=42684.

11  Stephen Edward Snyder, "Urban and Rural Divergence in Mortality Trends: A Comment on Case and Deaton," *Proceedings of the National Academy of Sciences* 113, no. 7 (February 2016), E815, http://www.pnas.org/content/113/7/E815.full. Anne Case and Sir Angus Deaton, "Mortality and Morbidity in the 21st Century," in *Brookings Papers on Economic Activity*, (Washington, DC: The Brookings Institution, 2017), https://www.brookings.edu/wp-content/uploads/2017/08/casetextsp17bpea.pdf.

12  Janet Adamy and Paul Overberg, "Rural America Is the New 'Inner City,'" *Wall Street Journal*, May 26, 2017, https://www.wsj.com/articles/rural-america-is-the-new-inner-city-1495817008.

13  U.S. Department of Agriculture, *Rural America at a Glance, 2015 Edition*.

14  Ibid.

15  Stephan J. Goetz, "Human Capital and Rural Labor Issues," *American Journal of Agricultural Economics* 75, no. 5 (1993), 1164–68.

16  Eleanor Krause and Richard V. Reeves, *Rural Dreams: Upward Mobility in America's Countryside*, Brookings Institution Center on Children and Families, September 2017, https://www.brookings.edu/wp-content/uploads/2017/08/es_20170905_ruralmobility.pdf.

17  See National Conference of State Legislatures, Education Bill Tracking Database, http://www.ncsl.org/research/education/education-bill-tracking-database.aspx.

18  Mary S. Hoffschwelle, *Rebuilding the Rural Southern Community: Reformers, Schools, and Homes in Tennessee, 1900–1930* (Knoxville: University of Tennessee Press, 1998), and David R. Reynolds, *There Goes the Neighborhood: Rural School Consolidation at the Grass Roots in Early Twentieth-Century Iowa* (Iowa City: University of Iowa Press, 2002).

19  Ibid.

20  Ibid.

21  Michael John Corbett, *Learning to Leave: The Irony of Schooling in a Coastal Community* (Nova Scotia, Canada: Fernwood, 2007); and Hernán Cuervo, *Understanding Social Justice in Rural Education* (Berlin: Springer, 2016).

22 Claudia Wallis, "Trump's Victory and the Politics of Resentment," *Scientific American*, November 12, 2016, https://www.scientificamerican.com/article/trump-s-victory-and-the-politics-of-resentment/.

23 Hoffschwelle, *Rebuilding the Rural Southern Community*; Campbell Scribner, "Beyond the Metropolis: The Forgotten History of Small-Town Teachers' Unions," *American Journal of Education* 121, no. 4 (August 2015), 531–61; and Mara Casey Tieken, *Why Rural Schools Matter* (Chapel Hill: University of North Carolina Press, 2014).

24 Gerald Gamm and Thad Kousser, "No Strength in Numbers: The Failure of Big-City Bills in American State Legislatures, 1880–2000," *American Political Science Review* 107, no. 4 (November 2013), 663–78.

25 Emily Badger, "As American as Apple Pie? The Rural Vote's Disproportionate Slice of Power," *New York Times*, November 20, 2016, https://www.nytimes.com/2016/11/21/upshot/as-american-as-apple-pie-the-rural-votes-disproportionate-slice-of-power.html; and Frances E. Lee and Bruce I. Oppenheimer, *Sizing Up the Senate: The Unequal Consequences of Equal Representation* (Chicago, IL: University of Chicago Press, 1999).

26 Note: *Baker v. Carr* was one of two Supreme Court cases that led to the current standard of "one person, one vote" in state legislative redistricting. See A. G. Sulzberger, "Rural Legislators' Power Ebbs as Populations Shift," *New York Times*, June 2, 2011, https://www.nytimes.com/2011/06/03/us/03rural.html.

27 Alan Greenblatt, "Rural Areas Lose People but Not Power," *Governing.com*, April 2014, http://www.governing.com/topics/politics/gov-rural-areas-lose-people-not-power.html.

28 Scribner, "Beyond the Metropolis."

29 Badger, "As American as Apple Pie?"

30 Tom W. Smith et al., "General Social Surveys, 1972–2016," National Science Foundation and NORC at the University of Chicago, accessed October 6, 2017, http://gssdataexplorer.norc.org.

31 *Washington Post* and Kaiser Family Foundation, *Survey of Rural America: Topline and Methodology*, June 2017, 5, https://www.washingtonpost.com/apps/g/page/national/washington-post-kaiser-family-foundation-rural-and-small-town-america-poll/2217/; and Jose A. DelReal and Scott Clement, "Poll of Rural Americans Shows Deep Cultural Divide with Urban Centers," *Washington Post*, June 17, 2017, https://www.washingtonpost.com/amphtml/classic-apps/new-poll-of-rural-americans-shows-deep-cultural-divide-with-urban-centers/2017/06/16/d166c31e-4189-11e7-9869-bac8b446820a_story.html.

32 *Washington Post* and Kaiser Family Foundation, *Survey of Rural America*, 14; and Smith et al., "General Social Surveys."

33 James Davison Hunter and Carl Desportes, "The Vanishing Center of American Democracy: The 2016 Survey of American Political Culture," Institute for Advanced Studies in Culture at the University of Virginia, 2016, http://www.iasc-culture.org/survey_archives/VanishingCenter.pdf.

34 *Washington Post* and Kaiser Family Foundation, *Survey of Rural America*, 5.

35  Ibid., 3–4.

36  Ibid.,19–20.

37  *Washington Post* and Kaiser Family Foundation, *Survey of Rural America*, 7.

38  Note: Author calculations. Data are from the NCES Local Education Agency Universe Survey, for the 2012–2013 school year. Presidential vote share at the county level is based on data collected by the *Guardian*. Only regular school districts and local components of supervisory unions that serve at least one operational school are included here. Charter schools and other special institutions are excluded from the tabulation. Both Hawaii and Alaska are excluded from the analysis; presidential-election returns for Alaska are not reported at the borough level (county equivalent).

39  Note: Author calculations. Data are from the NCES Local Education Agency Universe Survey, for the 2014–2015 school year. Presidential vote share at the county level is based on data gathered by Townhall.com. Only regular school districts and local components of supervisory unions that serve at least one operational school are included here. Charter schools and other special institutions are excluded from the tabulation. Both Hawaii and Alaska are excluded from the analysis; presidential-election returns are not reported at the borough level (county equivalent).

40  Clarence N. Stone, Jeffrey R. Henig, Bryan D. Jones, and Carol Pierannunzi, *Building Civic Capacity: The Politics of Reforming Urban Schools* (Lawrence: University Press of Kansas, 2001).

41  U.S. Department of Education, "Characteristics of Public School Districts in the United States: Results from the 2007–08," 11, Table 5, http://files.eric.ed.gov/fulltext/ED505835.pdf.

42  Scribner, "Beyond the Metropolis."

43  U.S. Department of Agriculture, *Rural America at a Glance, 2016 Edition.*

44  John Reinan and J. Patrick Coolican, "Funding for Schools Pits Farmers against City Dwellers in Rural Minnesota," February 4, 2017, *Star Tribune*, http://www.startribune.com/funding-for-schools-pits-farmers-against-city-dwellers-in-rural-minnesota/412791823/#1; Matt Sanctis, "Farmers Face Skyrocketing Taxes, Increases Could Affect Schools," *Springfield News-Sun*, November 3, 2014, http://www.springfieldnewssun.com/news/local/farmers-face-skyrocketing-taxes-increases-could-affect-schools/d5yYNK22XAPNhYMZVyVbWN/; and Sam Milton, "Ohio Farmers' Plea for Lower Property Tax Could Adversely Affect Schools," *Education Week*, June 6, 2016, http://blogs.edweek.org/edweek/rural_education/2016/06/ohio_farmers_pleas_for_lower_property_tax_could_adversely_affect_schools.html.

45  Janice C. Probst, Michael E. Samuels, Kristen P. Jespersen, Karin Willert, R. Suzanne Swann, and Joshua A. McDuffie, *Minorities in Rural America: An Overview of Population Characteristics* (Columbia: University of South Carolina, 2002).

46  Daniel T. Lichter, "Immigration and the New Racial Diversity in Rural America," *Rural Sociology* 77, no. 1 (2012), 3–35, https://www.ncbi.nlm.nih.gov/pmc/articles/PMC4606139/.

47  U.S. Census Bureau, "A Comparison of Rural and Urban America: Household Income and Poverty," December 8, 2016, https://www.census.gov/newsroom/blogs/random-samplings/2016/12/a_comparison_of_rura.html.

48  Abigail Hausllohner and Emily Guskin, "Differences, in Black and White: Rural Americans' Views Often Set Apart by Race," *Washington Post*, June 19, 2017, https://www.washingtonpost.com/national/differences-in-black-and-white-rural-americans-views-often-set-apart-by-race/2017/06/16/9e3b8164–47c9–11e7-a196-a1bb629f64cb_story.html.

49  Patricia S. Kusimo, "Rural Americans and Education: The Legacy of the Brown Decision," Eric Digests, 1999, https://www.ericdigests.org/1999-3/brown.htm.

50  Sabrina Hope King, "The Limited Presence of African-American Teachers," *Review of Educational Research* 63, no. 2 (June 1993), 115–49; and Deirdre Oakley, Jacob Stowell, and John R. Logan, "The Impact of Desegregation on Black Teachers in the Metropolis, 1970–2000," *Ethnic Racial Studies* 39, no. 9 (2009), 1576–98.

51  Lichter, "Immigration and the New Racial Diversity."

52  Orfield and Frankenberg, *The Last Have Become First*; and Jeremy E. Fiel, "Decomposing School Resegregation Social Closure, Racial Imbalance, and Racial Isolation," *American Sociological Review* 78, no. 5 (October 2013), 828–48.

53  Daniel T. Lichter and Kenneth M. Johnson, "Immigrant Gateways and Hispanic Migration to New Destinations," *International Migration Review* 43, no. 3 (September 2009), 496–518.

54  Paul Manna, *School's In: Federalism and the National Education Agenda* (Washington, DC: Georgetown University Press, 2006).

55  Paul DiPerna and Andrew D. Catt, "2016 Schooling in America Survey: Public Opinion on K-12 Education and School Choice," EdChoice, October 2016, https://www.edchoice.org/research/2016-schooling-america-survey/.

56  Jackie Mader, "Rural Schools Struggle with SIG Transformation Model, Report Says," *Education Week*, September 7, 2016, http://blogs.edweek.org/edweek/rural_education/2016/09/rural_schools_struggle_with_sig_transformation_model_report_says.html.

57  Gallup, "Understanding Perspectives on Public Education in the US: The Gallup 2016 Survey of K-12 School District Superintendents," 2016, http://news.gallup.com/reports/195149/superintendent-report-2016.aspx#.

58  Ibid.

59  Marilyn Tallerico and Joan N. Burstyn, "Retaining Women in the Superintendency: The Location Matters," *Educational Administration Quarterly* 32, no. 1 Supplemental (1996), 642–64.

60  L. Harmon Ziegler and M. Kent Jennings, *Governing American Schools: Political Interaction in Local School Districts* (North Scituate, MA: Duxbury, 1974), 176.

61  Tallerico and Burstyn, "Retaining Women in the Superintendency."

62  See, for example, Diane Broncaccio, "Massachusetts Rural School Coalition Seeks More State Aid," *Daily Hampshire Gazette*, September 29, 2016, http://www.gazettenet.com/Rural-schools-mull-how-to-make-state-aware-of-budget-woes-5061982.

63  See, for example, Julie Chang and Dan Keemahill, "How Rural Lawmakers Killed School Choice Legislation in Texas," *My Statesman*, April 14, 2017, http://www.mystatesman.com/news/state—regional-govt—politics/how-rural-lawmakers-killed-school-choice-legislation-texas/3ADj4LG3TZ4mHOSHKUV 2cM/.

64  Jackie Mader, "School Administrators More Likely to Leave Rural Districts, Report Says," *Education Week*, August 25, 2016, http://blogs.edweek.org/ edweek/rural_education/2016/08/school_administrators_more_likely_to_leave_ rural_districts_report_says.html.

65  Jason A. Grissom and Stephanie Andersen, "Why Superintendents Turn Over," *American Educational Research Journal* 49, no. 6 (2012), 1146–80.

*Chapter 5*

# Rural Poverty and the Federal Safety Net: Implications for Rural Educators

Angela Rachidi

Perhaps the greatest challenge for rural schools serving poor children today is the same as the challenge in urban settings: ensuring that poor children receive a high-quality education that equips them for future success. Although poverty is often viewed as a distinctly urban problem, rural residents experience it too, often struggling with the same underlying conditions including joblessness, substance abuse, and single parenthood. Without a doubt, such conditions affect a child's ability to learn and thrive in school, and impoverished communities often cannot support good schools.

School remains the best path out of poverty for rural children, but its role is challenged by the problems poverty creates. The surest way to address this challenge is to understand poverty and its principle causes. Doing so will ensure that education remains an escape from poverty toward opportunity.

For economic opportunity to be a reality for poor rural children, they need to overcome many obstacles. One of the most important institutions to combat these challenges is school, which increasingly must serve as a support system to struggling families at the same time it offers education as a path upward. This places rural educators in a bind: if they focus too much attention on social services, their ability to educate is strained; but if they focus too little attention, educating poor children becomes difficult. While schools and educators cannot possibly be expected to address all the underlying causes of poverty, they certainly have a role to play.

For rural schools and educators to meet this challenge, rural areas need a safety net that supports low-income families (especially in their ability to sustain employment) so that children can thrive at home and schools can focus on educating. Rural educators can help achieve this by coordinating with local social service agencies, communicating with families about benefits available to them, and ensuring that the struggles of children's home lives are taken into account when dealing with them at school. But these efforts can still be challenging when faced with a rural population that dislikes or even mistrusts government intervention, often with good reason.

Government programs are typically designed to help those with little to no income, possibly creating disincentives to work or stigma associated with those who do receive benefits. This is why rural schools and safety net programs alone cannot fully solve the problem of rural poverty. Economic development efforts that strengthen the local labor market, combined with government and education efforts, are needed.

In the following pages, the challenges faced by rural schools and educators in addressing poverty are reviewed. Poverty rates for rural versus urban areas are described, along with trends over time. Next, the underlying conditions associated with poverty and the prevalence of these factors in rural areas are reviewed. Then, a description of the federal government's main safety net programs for the poor, along with the extent to which they serve rural populations are documented. And finally, the implications of both poverty and its underlying conditions on rural schools and educators are discussed, with a few broad recommendations aimed at helping rural schools and educators serve poor rural children and their families.


## RURAL VERSUS URBAN POVERTY

Understanding poverty in rural areas runs into two challenges. The first involves differences in how urban and rural are defined, which changes the understanding of poverty depending on which definition is used. Nonmetropolitan areas (often used to depict rural areas) have higher poverty rates than do metropolitan areas, but this trend is reversed when considering urban and rural areas as defined by the U.S. Census Bureau. Poverty rates using both definitions are considered in this chapter.

The second challenge is in the definition of poverty, which again alters the picture depending on what measure is used. The official poverty rate uses the same threshold—the line that delineates who is poor—for the entire United States, which fails to factor in different costs of living by geography. Income for a family living in New York City is treated the same as income for a family in rural Mississippi, even though the New York family likely needs more income to achieve the same living standards as the Mississippi family.

To address this concern, the Census Bureau began publishing the Supplemental Poverty Measure in 2010, which adjusts the threshold geographically based on the local cost of living. Additionally, the supplemental measure considers pretax or noncash government benefits, such as the Earned Income Tax

Credit (EITC) or food benefits. In many ways the supplemental poverty measure is superior to the official measure, and both are presented in this chapter.

Figure 5.1 shows official poverty rates using the metropolitan definition of urban and rural areas. As shown, poverty rates have consistently been higher in nonmetropolitan areas compared to metropolitan areas since the 1960s. In the time since President Lyndon Johnson's "War on Poverty" in the 1960s, nonmetropolitan poverty declined dramatically, but has remained at roughly 15 percent since then and has always been higher in nonmetropolitan areas than metropolitan ones.

Many factors contributed to this large rural decline in poverty throughout the 1960s, including increased federal spending on safety net programs, such as Medicaid and Medicare, economic development opportunities that moved south, and poor Southern residents moving north or into cities.

This trend holds across age groups, including among children. In 2015, the official poverty rate among children was 24.3 percent in nonmetropolitan areas compared to a metropolitan rate of 20.1 percent (figure 5.2).

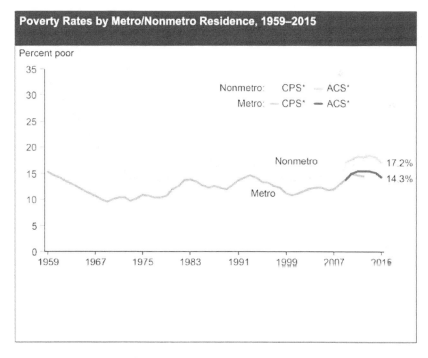

**Figure 5.1   Poverty Rates by Metro/Nonmetro Residence, 1959–2015.** *Source:* Calculated by USDA, Economic Research Service using data from the U.S. Census Bureau's Current Population Survey (CPS) 1960-2013 American Community Survey (ACS) estimates for 2009–2015

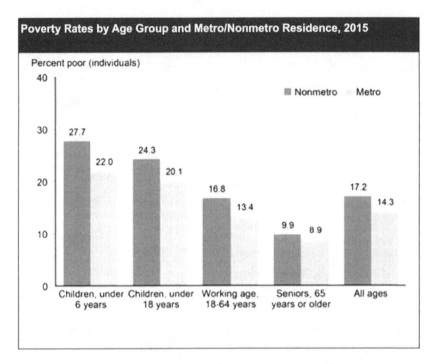

Figure 5.2   **Poverty Rates by Age Group and Metro/Nonmetro Residence, 2015.** *Source:*
**USDA, Economic Research Service using data from the U.S. Census Bureau,
American Community Survey, 2015**

However, the Census Bureau's definition of rurality (rather than metropolitan and nonmetropolitan) reveals a slightly different picture, with poverty in
rural areas lower than that of urban areas (figure 5.3). According to the most
recent data, urban poverty was almost 3 percentage points higher than in rural
areas, including among children (figure 5.3).

Consideration of the supplemental poverty measure provides yet another
picture of poverty. Again, the supplemental poverty measure adjusts the
threshold based on geography and in general lowers the threshold in rural
areas compared to urban areas. It also considers all government benefits
income, including tax-based and noncash income. Primarily because of the
lower threshold, nonmetropolitan poverty is lower than metropolitan poverty
when utilizing the supplemental measure, although the gap has narrowed in
recent years (figure 5.4).

Poverty's implications for rural educators remain the same no matter the
poverty measure or definition of rurality that is used. It is important to understand rural poverty rates, as well as the corresponding measurement issues, in
order to fully grasp how to address it. The data mentioned earlier show that

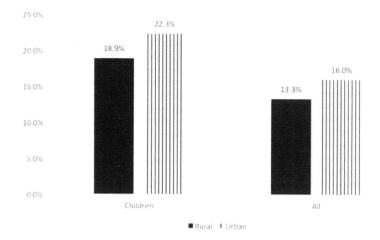

Figure 5.3    Official Poverty Rates in Rural versus Urban Areas, U.S. Census Bureau
Definition. *Source:* U.S. Census Bureau, 2011–2015 American Community
Survey

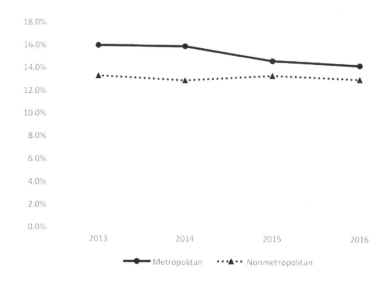

Figure 5.4    Supplemental Poverty Rates for All Individuals. *Source:* U.S. Census Bureau
Current Population Survey, https://www.census.gov/content/dam/Census/
library/publications/2017/demo/p60-261.pdf

poverty in rural areas is likely lower than urban ones, but only slightly, suggesting that rural areas deserve as much attention as urban when it comes to combating poverty. This requires understanding the underlying conditions of rural poverty, the federal government's response to it, and how it affects rural schools.

## UNDERLYING CONDITIONS OF RURAL POVERTY

Rural schools and educators must understand the underlying issues associated with poverty for them to meet the needs of poor, rural children. To the extent that social and cultural factors unique to rural environments contribute to poverty, policymakers must tailor their approaches accordingly. Increasingly, however, rural areas in America are experiencing the same underlying conditions as urban areas, suggesting that solutions can be shared.

In search of solutions, Jennifer Sherman, in her 2009 book, *Those Who Work, Those Who Don't: Poverty, Morality, and Family in Rural America*, argues that rural communities have declined in recent years primarily because existing economic and political climates (e.g., reduced employment, stagnated wages, declining union membership) made them feel powerless and helpless. In response, they revised their own moral foundations, which led to behaviors typically seen in urban areas, such as substance abuse, single parenthood, and the declining role of men in communal and family life.[1]

Rural residents might also be more inclined to reject government help when facing poverty given the stigma involved and the close-knit nature of many small towns, adding to their despair. Add to that a less sophisticated human service infrastructure in rural compared to urban areas, and rural residents may feel particularly helpless.

Perhaps this is even truer today. In 2015, economists Anne Case and Angus Deaton of Princeton identified a concerning trend of rising mortality and morbidity among middle-aged non-Hispanic whites.[2] Since then, their research has led to a better understanding of these "deaths of despair," which they found stem from rising substance use and suicides among non-Hispanic whites. Although they acknowledge that the problem is endemic to both urban and rural areas, the spread to rural areas raises new concerns about how social and economic issues translate to health and well-being.

Demographic comparisons of rural and urban populations further contribute to our understanding of these social and economic issues, suggesting that rural populations might be worse off in some ways than urban populations. According to the U.S. Census Bureau definition of rurality, rural residents are less educated than urban residents, with only 20 percent possessing a bachelor's degree or more, compared to 29 percent of urban residents.

Unsurprisingly, this translates into a smaller share of working-age adults (age eighteen to sixty-four) in rural areas being employed (67 percent versus 70 percent). A larger share, however, is married (62 percent versus 51 percent), and the higher marriage rate among rural residents also translates to a higher percentage of children living in married-couple households in rural areas, yet almost 25 percent still live with one or more unmarried parents.[3]

As rural educators think about how to address poverty among their students, they must consider the underlying conditions. Four specific factors are worth exploring in more detail: work status, education level, family structure, and immigration.

## Work Status

For people of employment age and their families, work is the primary source of income. Naturally, people who work less are more likely to be in poverty. Fortunately, working and still being poor is rather uncommon, but still important. Slack analyzed the working poor by metropolitan status and found that from the early 1980s to 2003 the percentage of all workers who were poor was around 5 percent with only a small variation, and nonmetropolitan areas consistently had a slightly higher share of working poor than metropolitan areas, although that gap got smaller across time.[4]

More recently, Thiede et al. explored the working poor through 2013 and found similar shares of all workers who were in poverty (approximately 5 percent).[5] However, they also found disparities based on various characteristics. Working women in nonmetropolitan areas were much more likely to be poor than their male counterparts, likely stemming from a concentration of low-wage, female-dominated jobs in rural areas, while the gap by gender was narrower in metropolitan areas.

Interestingly, the gap between white and black poverty rates was larger in metropolitan areas than nonmetropolitan areas, but the gap in the poverty rates between white and Hispanic workers in nonmetropolitan areas was much larger than in metropolitan areas, possibly a result of the agricultural economy more present in nonmetropolitan areas, which employs many Hispanic immigrants.

Explored another way, the metropolitan–nonmetropolitan divide remains when considering the share of the poor who work, but it has changed over the past fifteen years. In the early 2000s, nonmetropolitan people in poverty were more likely to be working at least half-time than those in metropolitan areas.[6] But by 2013, this trend reversed and poor people in nonmetropolitan areas had a work rate (at least half-time) that was 4 percentage points below that of poor people in metropolitan areas (23.6 percent versus 28 percent, respectively).

It is possible that this shift is due to labor market deterioration in rural areas, but it could also be the result of a declining labor supply in terms of people with higher education levels moving out of rural areas leaving those with limited education and limited prospects behind. The result is that not only does this show that poor people in nonmetropolitan areas work less than their metropolitan counterparts, but also the vast majority (more than 75 percent) work less than half-time.[7]

## Education Level

Education level and work status are strongly linked. Those with limited education are less likely to work, which in turn makes them more likely to be in poverty. Nonmetropolitan residents are less educated on average than metropolitan residents, which likely helps explain why a smaller share of nonmetropolitan working-age adults eighteen to sixty-four work (67.6 percent) compared to metropolitan adults,[8] although it's possible that age still plays a role, with rural populations being older on average than urban populations.

In rural and urban areas, those with lower levels of education have higher rates of poverty, but the least educated in nonmetropolitan areas are in poverty at slightly lower rates than their metropolitan counterparts, perhaps because they work more hours.

## Labor Market

Also strongly related to the working share of the population is the local labor market. Since 2000, the nonmetropolitan population has grown slightly (approximately 5 percent) but total employment has declined.[9] This contrasts with metropolitan areas, which have experienced population and employment growth since 2000. This could be the result of changing demographics and other population-based factors, but it is also a function of the local labor market.

While service-related industries dominate both metropolitan and nonmetropolitan areas, goods-producing sectors, such as farming, forestry, and manufacturing, are much more common in nonmetropolitan areas. This means that as these sectors decline as a share of all industries, it disproportionately affects nonmetropolitan areas. And as jobs in these sectors are replaced by lower-paying service jobs, fewer "good" employment opportunities exist in nonmetropolitan areas.

Economist David Autor argues that trade policy has directly affected these areas by causing employment to decline, resulting in an increase in transfer payments such as unemployment insurance and disability claims. Others describe the geography of the rise in disability claims in recent years and note that claims are concentrated in the rural south, and that increases in claims are highly correlated with lost job opportunities.

Changes like these are important not only from an economic perspective, but also because the labor market directly contributes to social cohesiveness and community. The types of jobs and industries present in a community help form personal and communal identities, and when those change, it may be difficult to adapt. One example is the 2017 book *Janesville: An American Story*, which profiled a town in Wisconsin that lost a General Motors plant in the mid-2000s. It describes the economic difficulties faced by laid-off workers, as well the difficulties faced by their families and neighborhoods as they adapted to a new identity not connected to the "local plant."[10]

Declines in other areas of social connectedness might contribute to feelings of isolation when major employers leave rural areas. As Robert Putnam wrote in his 2000 book, *Bowling Alone*, Americans in general (not only in rural areas) have become increasingly disconnected from each other as community institutions have disappeared.[11] As fewer identity-forming opportunities exist, it may be difficult for laid-off employees to adapt to life without a job, even aside from the lack of employment itself.

## Immigration

Immigration presents both challenges and opportunities to rural areas. On one hand, immigrants provide needed labor, which bolsters the local economy. On the other hand, they introduce a different culture that may be hard to adapt to for native-born residents. Immigrants can also present challenges to local schools when English is not the primary language spoken at home.

Urban areas might be more equipped to adapt to these challenges given the existence of a higher concentration of immigrants, but rural areas also experience immigration's challenges. Many immigrants settle in rural America, but because rural areas provide a more isolated existence they often go unnoticed. According to U.S. Census data, 25 percent of the rural population is nonwhite (although not all immigrants).[12]

Increased poverty is another reality when it comes to immigration. While America provides economic opportunity for immigrants from poor countries, some come here with few skills but a willingness to work hard in low-wage jobs, which drives up poverty. Immigrants tend to have higher poverty rates than their native-born counterparts, largely because of lower education levels, suggesting that as immigration increases in rural areas, so too will poverty.

But increased immigration in rural areas and its relationship with poverty is complex. While immigrants have higher poverty rates, their impact can also be positive because they display higher work rates and marriage rates than native-born Americans. For this reason, immigration may contribute to higher poverty rates in rural areas, but not necessarily the associated social and familial decay.

## Looking to the Future

Many of these trends have been building for years, suggesting that rural areas will continue to experience challenges into the future. The association between employment, limited education, labor market changes, and immigration is strong and there is little indication that current trends will reverse. Efforts are needed at the federal and local levels to address these challenges if rural populations are to have ample opportunity to thrive.

## FEDERAL RESPONSE TO RURAL POVERTY

Rural schools cannot be expected to confront these underlying conditions alone. Fortunately, a number of programs exist at the federal level to address challenges associated with poverty and low income across America. However, federal anti-poverty programs are complex and often confusing. To get a sense of how much, simply consider that over eighty programs exist to serve the needs of low-income families and individuals, and each program is designed differently, often with little coordination between programs.

For example, some are almost completely federally financed and administered, while others are financed by the federal government but administered by states. Still others receive some federal funding but states are required to share in the costs. Additionally, some are administered through the tax system, while others are administered at the local level through state or county social service offices.

Due to the variance in how these programs are financed and operated, states and local areas have varying levels of control over the design of and access to programs, meaning that services may look very different in rural areas compared to urban areas. Even between different rural areas, programs can look very different.

For example, anti-poverty programs can have different eligibility criteria and varying means of access depending on where one lives. Rural areas might face particular challenges in designing programs accessible to their constituents because of the dispersed population. While this creates challenges for rural areas, it also creates opportunity because rural schools and other community stakeholders can collaborate with social service agencies to design programs that meet the unique needs of their community.

Recognizing the distinct challenges faced by rural areas in accessing social services, the federal government has engaged several efforts directly targeting rural areas. The Department of Health and Human Services (HHS) houses the National Advisory Committee on Rural Health and Human Services, which advises HHS on a host of issues important to rural areas. Additionally, President Barack Obama established the White House Rural Council in 2009 to advise federal efforts in rural areas.

Increasing the ability of poor families to access social services is a critical step in ensuring that children receive necessary services, so they can thrive at home and in school. Yet, many rural populations are skeptical of government programs or reluctant to accept help. For this reason, government programs should not be pushed onto low-income families, but at the same time, access should be available for families who want and need services.

While many programs serve rural populations, access to a few in particular plays an outsized role, and those programs are worth mentioning in more depth. The extent to which poor rural families and their children receive these benefits may be the difference in how well their child performs in school. Health insurance, food, and income assistance through the EITC have all been shown to positively affect child health and well-being. For this reason, school officials and educators have a stake in understanding these programs, as well as helping their students access them to the extent that their families want them.

The largest, and perhaps most critical of programs, is public health insurance. Medicaid is the country's primary public health insurance program for low-income populations, along with the Children's Health Insurance Program (CHIP), which covers children not covered by Medicaid. Medicaid and CHIP provide health insurance coverage to approximately 74 million people per month, and Medicaid alone costs the federal government over $545 billion per year.[13]

Medicaid and CHIP can be particularly helpful to residents of rural areas, as they generally have lower employment levels and lower-wage jobs than people in urban areas, meaning they are less likely to have employer-provided coverage or to afford coverage on their own. According to the Kaiser Family Foundation, rural residents are less likely to receive employer-provided coverage, with 61 percent of people in rural areas with health coverage receiving employer-provided coverage compared to 64 percent in urban areas.[14] Beyond those who have health insurance coverage, rural populations are slightly more likely to be uninsured. In 2015, 12 percent of rural residents were uninsured compared to 10 percent in urban areas.[15]

Medicaid has been very effective at providing health insurance to those who otherwise would not have it. The uninsured rate declined in all areas where Medicaid was expanded as part of the Affordable Care Act (ACA), and the decline was attributed more to Medicaid than expansions to private coverage.[16] In terms of health outcomes, most agree that increased health insurance coverage leads to better health. But problems remain with the overall cost of Medicaid, its efficiency, and whether it creates negative work incentives. Notwithstanding these problems, ensuring that low-income children in rural areas have access to health insurance is an important goal.

After Medicaid, the Supplemental Nutrition Assistance Program (SNAP), known before 2008 as the Food Stamp Program, is the second-largest need-tested program for low-income families in the United States. In the average month in 2016, it served 44.2 million people and in recent years has cost the federal government approximately $74 billion per year.[17] It covers approximately 14 percent of the entire population, and 83 percent of eligible households participated according to the most recent data.[18]

A large body of research shows that SNAP reduces poverty, improves food security among low-income households, and positively affects infant health and benefits children in the long run.[19] Rural families in particular benefit a great deal from SNAP. According to the Center for Rural Affairs, 14.6 percent of rural households receive SNAP—a larger share than both metropolitan and micropolitan areas.[20] Households with children and households with senior citizens receiving SNAP benefits are more common in rural areas compared to urban areas, and participation among eligible households is higher in rural areas.[21]

Again, however, problems associated with SNAP, such as work disincentives, poor nutrition controls, and program integrity, undermine its potential. Nonetheless, it remains an important resource for low-income families and communities to ensure that the nutritional needs of children are being met, even though improvements to the program are needed.

Closely related to SNAP is the National School Lunch Program, which serves free and reduced-cost lunches to low-income children in school. According to U.S. Census data, 22.4 percent of rural households have a child who benefits from the National School Lunch Program. Similar to SNAP, the National School Lunch Program has been shown to benefit children who participate in it, increasing consumption of fruits and vegetables among students, without leading to increased weight gain or obesity.[22] With 1.4 million rural households with children participating in the National School Lunch Program, it provides a needed safety net that increases healthy eating for poor children.

The EITC is another anti-poverty program that assists a large share of low-income rural residents. It is the third-largest government transfer for low-income families in the United States, behind Medicaid and SNAP; in tax year 2013, $68.1 billion was distributed to more than 28 million tax filers.[23] Unlike most income-transfer programs that provide monthly or even more frequent benefits, the EITC is a refundable tax credit, which means it is provided to low-income households once per year. Because most EITC-eligible tax filers owe little to no income tax, most beneficiaries receive the credit as a refund.

Approximately one-quarter of all EITC claims go to tax filers in rural areas,[24] and among all rural tax filers, 22 percent receive the EITC.[25] Since the EITC only goes to working families, it is particularly helpful for workers in rural areas who face declining wages and opportunities to pursue higher-paying jobs.

Although not specific to rural areas, reviews of the literature have found the EITC to be effective, with the family EITC linked to increased employment rates of single mothers and poverty reduction for millions of families. The EITC has been particularly effective at improving children's outcomes, including positive impacts on academic achievement and high school graduation, as well as better child behavior and adult health outcomes.[26]

Across these four programs alone, the government provides substantial resources to low-income families in rural areas. According to analysis of 2011–2015 U.S. Census data, approximately 40 percent of nonmetropolitan households in the bottom 10 percent of the income distribution received SNAP benefits, 36 percent received the EITC, and almost 60 percent received public health insurance coverage.[27]

Program coverage in nonmetropolitan areas among the poorest households shows that many already access government benefits. Enacting reforms that make programs even more effective, while also ensuring that eligible households that want benefits can access them, can help children perform better in school.

## IMPLICATIONS FOR RURAL SCHOOLS AND EDUCATORS

By witnessing it each school day, rural educators are acutely aware of the consequences of poverty for their students. And they are also no doubt aware of the research on the struggles that low-income children have in schools. As Sean Reardon argued in 2013, referring to the gap in outcomes between low- and higher-income children,

> If we do not find ways to reduce the growing inequality in education outcomes, we are in danger of bequeathing our children a society in which the American Dream—the promise that one can rise, through education and hard work, to any position in society—is no longer a reality. Our schools cannot be expected to solve this problem on their own, but they must be part of the solution.[28]

Research suggests that low-income student academic achievement is not necessarily due to differences in teacher effectiveness across low- and high-income students,[29] reinforcing Reardon's view that schools cannot be expected to solve the problem alone. But schools inevitably play a role given that it is likely the only institution that comes into contact with almost all poor children at some point. And evidence from high-performing, high-poverty schools confirms that given the right tools, teachers can help students in high-poverty areas learn and thrive.[30]

If low-income students receive similar levels of quality instruction as their higher-income counterparts, then other factors must explain their lower performance. Understanding these other factors is important for establishing policies both inside and outside the school that might help student achievement. Schools and educators must work with the broader policy community to understand the dynamics outside of school that lead to performance, and work together to address those issues.

The negative effects of low income and the stresses of poverty on children are well documented. In their seminal review of the literature, Brooks-Gunn and Duncan described the substantial role that family income played in explaining child outcomes, particularly academic achievement.[31] Of particular concern was their finding that experiencing poverty in the early years led to worse outcomes than later in adolescence, suggesting that intervening early is crucial.

Child poverty has been shown to affect brain development and subsequently lower academic achievement, requiring that any public policies designed to better serve low-income children must focus on the early years. But what can rural schools do to address poverty and low income in their communities? Three broad focus areas are suggested.

First, rural families and schools should leverage federal safety net programs to the extent possible and to the extent that it serves either as temporary assistance during times of unemployment or as a work support. One downside of increasing access to government safety net programs, even though programs positively affect children, is that it might lead to increased family dependency on government and further community decline. This is why economic development efforts and policies that increase employment among parents must accompany any efforts to increase access to safety net programs.

Rural schools can help by sharing information and coordinating with their local social service agencies. For example, all recipients of the school lunch program should be assessed for SNAP eligibility and vice versa. Yet some schools and social service agencies might not share this information with each other. Doing so might increase receipt of these benefits among eligible families.

Second, broader policy efforts are needed in rural areas to address the underlying causes of poverty, particularly those that affect employment. This is beyond the scope of what schools and educators can achieve alone, but they play a critical role in preparing students for the workforce, as well as serving as a community resource for struggling families. Schools should look to partner with workforce development agencies to offer resources to unemployed parents, as well as focusing on preparing their students for jobs.

Third, the psychological stress of poverty is linked to poor academic performance among low-income students. This stress can be amplified by joblessness and fragile family life—experiences that children bring to school. As identified earlier, a larger share of rural populations may experience these underlying conditions than do those in other geographic settings.

While schools are not equipped to solve all family-life problems, recognizing them and adapting student disciplinary policies may be one place to start. As noted in a 2012 issue of *Rural Policy Matters*, research shows that schools still use disparate discipline policies depending on the student group.[32] More research is needed to compare disciplinary actions with low-income compared to high-income students, as well as rural versus urban. If low-income students are disproportionately disciplined, review of these policies might be in order.

Finally, beyond what is possible for rural educators and schools, rural areas must also focus on economic development efforts that attract jobs and educationally diverse people. Widely reported after the 2010 decennial census, the American population has shifted toward urban areas over the past two decades. As younger, educated people leave rural areas for cities, rural towns struggle to replace the resources that they used to bring. State governments must focus economic development attention on rural areas that factor in the changing demographics of rural residents, as well as work to attract higher-educated residents.

## CONCLUSION

The best available data suggest that rural areas have at least the same level of poverty as urban areas, along with similar underlying conditions. Problems associated with joblessness, single parenthood, low education, and substance abuse are perhaps as common in rural areas as they are in urban areas. Attention to these issues is important for rural schools and educators because they make it more difficult to educate rural students and help them meet their potential.

The federal government offers a number of safety net programs to help alleviate economic hardship among low-income families, many of which have an evidence base of effectiveness. Access to these safety net programs is important, but longer-term economic opportunity is critical and can only be achieved in concert with family and community. Rural schools can help by coordinating with local social service agencies to ensure that families receive the supports that they might need, but they can also help increase economic opportunities for those in the community.

While rural schools should not be expected to solve all the problems associated with poverty, they have a responsibility to recognize the challenges low-income students face and do what they can to help alleviate some of those challenges. Beyond that, rural communities, and the government agencies that serve them, must recognize that government programs cannot be the entire solution. Economic-development efforts that bring jobs and people back to rural areas must also play a role.

## NOTES

1 Jennifer Sherman, *Those Who Work, Those Who Don't: Poverty, Morality, and Family in Rural America* (Minneapolis: University of Minnesota Press, 2009).

2 Anne Case and Angus Deaton, "Rising Morbidity and Mortality in Midlife among White Non-Hispanic Americans in the 21st Century," *Proceedings of the National Academy of Sciences* 112, no. 49 (December 2015), 15078–83.

3 U.S. Census Bureau, "Measuring America," May 2, 2107, https://www.census.gov/library/measuring-america.html.

4 Tim Slack, "Working Poverty across the Metro-Nonmetro Divide: A Quarter Century in Perspective, 1979–2003," *Rural Sociology* 75, no. 3 (June 2010), 363–87.

5 Brian C. Thiede, Daniel T. Lichter, and Tim Slack, "Working, but Poor: The Good Life in Rural America?" *Journal of Rural Studies* 59, (2016), 183–93.

6 Ibid.

7 Ibid.

8 Ibid.

9 U.S. Department of Agriculture, "Rural America at a Glance," 2016 Edition, https://www.ers.usda.gov/webdocs/publications/80894/eib-162.pdf?v=42684.

10 Amy Goldstein, *Janesville: An American Story* (New York: Simon & Schuster, 2018).

11 Robert Putnam, *Bowling Alone* (New York: Simon & Schuster, 2001).

12 Julia Foutz et al., "The Role of Medicaid in Rural America," The Henry J. Kaiser Family Foundation, April 25, 2017, https://www.kff.org/medicaid/issue-brief/the-role-of-medicaid-in-rural-america/.

13 Kaiser Family Foundation, https://www.kff.org/health-reform/state-indicator/total-monthly-medicaid-and-chip-enrollment/?currentTimeframe=0&sortModel=%7B%22colId%22:%22Location%22,%22sort%22:%22asc%22%7D.

14 Foutz et al., "The Role of Medicaid."

15 Ibid.

16 Rachel Garfield, "The Coverage Gap: Uninsured Poor Adults in States That Do Not Expand Medicaid," The Henry J. Kaiser Family Foundation, November 1, 2017, https://www.kff.org/uninsured/issue-brief/the-coverage-gap-uninsured-poor-adults-in-states-that-do-not-expand-medicaid/.

17 U.S. Department of Agriculture, "Food and Nutrition Service, SNAP Participation Summary," accessed December 7, 2017, https://fns-prod.azureedge.net/sites/default/files/pd/SNAP summary.pdf.

18 Karen E. Cunnyngham, "Reaching Those in Need: Estimates of State Supplemental Nutrition Assistance Program Participation Rates in 2012," U.S. Department of Agriculture Food and Nutrition Service and Mathematica Policy Research, February 2015, http://www.fns.usda.gov/sites/default/files/ops/Reaching2012.pdf.

19 Judith Bartfield et al., *SNAP Matters: How Food Stamps Affect Health and Well-Being* (Redwood City, CA: Stanford University Press, November 2015); Cunnyham, "Reaching Those in Need, 2012"; Douglas Almond, Hilary W. Hoynes, and Diane Whitmore Schanzenbach, "Inside the War on Poverty: The Impact of Food Stamps on Birth Outcomes," *Review of Economics and Statistics* 93, no. 2 (May 2011), 387–403, http://www.mitpressjournals.org/doi/abs/10.1162/REST_a_00089; and Hilary Hoynes, Diane Whitmore Schanzenbach, and Douglas Almond, "Long-Run Impacts of Childhood Access to the Safety Net," *American Economic Review* 106, no. 4 (April 2016), 903–34, https://www.aeaweb.org/articles?id=10.1257/aer.20130375.

20 Jon M. Bailey, "Supplemental Nutrition Assistance Program and Rural Households," Center for Rural Affairs, 2014, http://files.cfra.org/pdf/snap-and-rural-households.pdf.

21 Ibid.

22 Julian M. Alston, "US Food and Nutrition Programs: Costs, Effectiveness, and Impact on Obesity," American Boondoggle: Fixing the 2012 Farm Bill, American Enterprise Institute, 2012, https://www.aei.org/wp-content/uploads/2012/04/-us-food-and-nutrition-programs-costs-effectiveness-and-impact-on-obesity_092514480719.pdf.

23 Internal Revenue Service, "SOI Tax Stats: Individual Statistical Tables by Size of Adjusted Gross Income," accessed December 7, 2017, www.irs.gov/uac/SOI-Tax-Stats—-Individual-Statistical-Tables-by-Size-of-Adjusted-Gross-Income.

24 Marybeth J. Mattingly and Elizabeth Kneebone, "Share of Tax Filers Claiming EITC Increases across States and Place Types between 2007 and 2010," Carsey Research Institute, University of New Hampshire, Issue Brief no. 57 (2012), http://scholars.unh.edu/cgi/viewcontent.cgi?article=1181&context=carsey.

25 Cecile Murray and Elizabeth Kneebone, "The Earned Income Tax Credit and the White Working Class," Brookings Institute: The Avenue, April 18, 2017, https://www.brookings.edu/blog/the-avenue/2017/04/18/the-earned-income-tax-credit-and-the-white-working-class/.

26 Michelle Maxfield, "The Effects of the Earned Income Tax Credit on Child Achievement and Long-Term Educational Attainment," ICS Monograph, September 2015, https://www.instituteforchildsuccess.org/publication/effects-earned-income-tax-credit-child-achievement-long-term-educational-attainment/; David H. Rehkopf, K. W. Strully, and W. H. Dow, "The Short-Term Impacts of the Earned Income Tax Credit Disbursement on Health," *International Journal of Epidemiology* 43, no. 6 (2014), 1884–94; and Rita Hamad and David Rehkopf, "Poverty and Child Development: A Longitudinal Study of the Impact of the Earned Income Tax Credit," *American Journal of Epidemiology* 183, no. 9 (2016), 775–84.

27 Rebecca Glauber and Andrew Schaefer, "Employment, Poverty, and Public Assistance in the Rural United States," Carsey Research Institute, University of New Hampshire, Issue Brief no. 126 (2012), https://carsey.unh.edu/publication/rural-us-assistance.

28 Ibid.

29 Eric Isenberg et al., "Do Low-Income Students Have Equal Access to Effective Teachers? Evidence from 26 Districts (Final Report)," conducted by Mathematica Policy Research for the U.S. Department of Education, Institute of Education Sciences, National Center for Education Evaluation and Regional Assistance, October 27, 2016, https://www.mathematica-mpr.com/our-publications-and-findings/publications/do-low-income-students-have-equal-access-to-effective-teachers-evidence-from-26-districts.

30 Patricia J. Kannapel and Stephen K. Clements, with Diana Taylor and Terry Hibpshman, *Inside the Black Box of High-Performing High-Poverty Schools* (Lexington, KY: Prichard Committee for Academic Excellence, 2005).

31 Jeanne Brooks-Gunn and Greg Duncan, "The Effects of Poverty on Children," *The Future of Children* 7, no. 2 (Summer/Fall 1997), 55–71.

32 The Schott Foundation, "Studies Continue to Show Disparate Impact," Rural Policy Matters, accessed December 7, 2017,http://www.ruraledu.org/articles.php?id=2956.

## Chapter 6

# School Finance in Rural America

## James V. Shuls

In 5–4 decision in 1973, the U.S. Supreme Court effectively stamped out the potential for future federal school-finance litigation.[1] The case was *San Antonio Independent School District v. Rodriguez.* The plaintiffs in the case claimed that Texas's school-funding system was unconstitutional under the equal protection clause of the Fourteenth Amendment of the U.S. Constitution.[2] The court ruled against the plaintiffs and created significant precedent by determining that education is not a fundamental right under the nation's constitution.

Following the case, school-finance litigation shifted to the state court systems. To date, school-funding systems have been challenged in forty-five states.[3] Most recently, the Kansas Supreme Court ruled the state's school-finance system unconstitutional in what can only be called a prolonged legal and legislative saga.

Each school-finance court case has hinged on the definition of either "adequacy" or "equity" and the specific requirements in the state's constitution. The Kansas case considered both issues. Adequacy typically refers to the level of education funding being enough to provide an education to each student who meets some specified level. Equity, on the other hand, delves into issues relating to spending disparities among school districts.

It should go without saying that these are incredibly important concepts to grasp when considering school finance. They are, however, incomplete when we discuss rural school finance in particular. Here we must understand issues regarding *economies of scale*, *property assessments*, *levy rates*, and *cost-of-living adjustments*, to name just a few. These factors impact the amount of money a school will receive to a huge degree. Leaving them out of the conversation is leaving much out of the school-funding story.

This chapter explains how school districts and policymakers must understand the myriad of issues surrounding rural school finance. This encompasses more than just understanding how state funding formulas work. It touches on the fundamental differences that make rural schools unique from suburban and urban schools.

Much of this analysis will rely on information from Missouri. The makeup of Missouri offers a great unit of analysis when considering rural schools (it's also my home state and thus the state I know best in terms of school finance). Missouri has two large urban areas and plenty of suburban school districts, but the bulk of the Show-Me State's school districts are rural.

First, this chapter provides a snapshot view of rural school spending to give a better picture of the circumstances at play. Then, some issues that make it difficult for rural school districts to fund their schools to greater levels, and how this situation leaves rural school districts in a precarious position when it comes to state policy discussions, are explored. The chapter concludes with some recommendations for state policymakers.

One recurring theme throughout this chapter is that school finance, particularly rural school finance, is often about trade-offs. This could probably be said about most public-policy issues, especially incredibly complex ones. Still, there is something more to this notion here; the trade-offs are not simply about priorities.

At issue is not simply deciding whether more money should be given to education than to other social services or whether more assistance should be provided to urban schools than to rural schools. The issues here get at inherent desires to provide an adequate education for all students and desires to promote equity. They also touch on notions of local control.

In effect, there is an inherent tension between these important ideals. If states allow for greater local control, they allow for the possibility that some school districts may not provide an adequate education and allow inequity to creep into the system. This isn't simply about priorities; it gets at fundamental beliefs about the nature and role of public education.

## SNAPSHOT VIEW OF RURAL SCHOOL FINANCE

There is a joke in astronomy that goes, "Define the universe and give two examples." As A. J. Meadows notes, "The joke, of course, hinges on the fact that the universe is defined as containing everything that exists."[4] The challenge of providing a snapshot view of rural school finance is almost as challenging. The problem is that there is no one dominant narrative when it comes to rural school finance. In many instances, rural school districts are the lowest-spending school districts in the state. At the same time, other rural school districts are among the highest-spending school districts. On average, rural schools spend less than their counterparts in urban and suburban areas.

A variety of factors create this variation, but the biggest factor in determining whether schools spend a lot or a little per pupil tends to be school size. Incredibly small rural schools spend a lot per pupil because they lack economies of scale; they are inefficient. This gets at the heart of the matter facing rural schools: discussions of economies of scale run headlong into discussions of local control. Should states allow very small school districts to exist? If so, should communities be subsidized when they choose to have inefficiently tiny school districts? Before digging into these questions further, it's important to first look at how rural schools compare financially to their suburban and urban counterparts.

One of the most common metrics for school district spending is per-pupil expenditures (PPEs). This figure takes into account all operating expenses, but does not typically consider expenses on capital and debt servicing. PPEs are often compared when looking at spending in high-poverty school districts and nearby affluent school districts. When policymakers, policy wonks, and journalists discuss inequity among school districts, they typically reference PPE. When considering rural school finance, it makes sense to compare the PPE of rural schools to other schools.

This chapter does so using urban-centric designations from the National Center for Education Statistics (NCES). The NCES sorts school communities into four categories: city, suburban, town, and rural. The key designations for this chapter are those used for town and rural areas, which lie outside of urbanized areas.[5] This chapter groups town and rural school districts together, as they share many of the same features and are often very different from their suburban and urban counterparts.

As noted earlier, rural schools can be among the highest- and lowest-spending districts in a state. This is the case in Missouri. Of the Show-Me State's 517 school districts, 7 of the 10 lowest-spending districts in 2016 were rural. Two were categorized as "town-fringe," and the final as "town-distant." Meanwhile, nine of the ten highest-spending districts, as measured by PPE, were rural school districts. The only nonrural district in the top ten, Clayton (suburb: large), is typically regarded as the wealthiest school district in the state—and for good reason.

Located just outside the city of St. Louis, Clayton hosts a large business sector with many high-paying, white-collar jobs. Fewer than 14 percent of the 2,500 students in the district qualify for free or reduced-price lunches. The district spends more than $18,000 per pupil, well above the state average of $10,437. Yet, the Clayton School District ranks only ninth in the state in PPE. The Craig R-III School District, with just 68 students, took the top honor, spending $21,595 per pupil. A similar story exists in almost every other state.

It is clear to see the impact enrollment has in these districts. The average enrollment in the ten lowest-spending districts is 864. Meanwhile, it is just 90 in the nine highest-spending rural districts (not including Clayton). The rural school districts with more students benefit from economies of scale.

Note that the PPE difference is quite staggering: the highest-spending district spends roughly 300 percent more than the lowest-spending district. However, this alone does not actually say anything about the quality of the education the students are receiving. The low-spending district may actually provide better educational options than the high-spending school districts and simply have a lower PPE by virtue of having more students.

In education, number of students is often used as a measure of productivity— perhaps even reductively. When schools educate more students with the same expenses, this can be thought of as a cost savings: the school is more "productive." Think of it like this. A school that spends $1,000,000 on each of its 100 students spends $10,000 per pupil. If the school were to add one additional student, the PPE would drop to $9,901. As long as the quality of education does not drop—and there is no reason to think that it would—it's considered a savings. The school has become more efficient.

From 1930 to 1972, there was a tremendous push for greater efficiency and school consolidation in American schools. During this time period, the number of school districts dropped from 128,000 to less than 17,000.[6] It was argued that this move to larger school districts would not just yield cost savings, but that it would actually increase the quality of education for students, as schools would be able to offer more courses at higher quality than before.

The small, rural school with only thirty high school students, for example, may not be able to hire a physics teacher. Through consolidation, however, the school may build a larger student body and be able to provide this opportunity for students.

Yet, decades of research on economies of scale has not been able to determine the exact right size of school districts. Given the incredible complexity of schooling, the various community needs, and emerging world of school choice in education, this may not even be possible. There is some consensus, however, that benefits, such as potential savings on overhead and administrative costs, may accrue as small school districts consolidate into larger ones.

In a review of the research, Andrews, Duncombe, and Yinger write, "Sizeable potential cost savings may exist by moving from a very small district (500 or less pupils) to a district with 2000–4000 pupils."[7] From this, it is easy to see why very small, rural schools tend to spend a lot of money per pupil.

Despite having some small rural school districts that spend a lot of money per pupil, the NCES data show that town and rural schools spend less, on average, than their counterparts in urban and suburban school districts.[8] Statistically, it is easy to see how this happens—as high-spending, but incredibly small school districts are included in the calculations with larger, low-spending rural districts. However, why do rural schools spend less per pupil, on average?

## FACTORS THAT IMPACT RURAL SCHOOL FINANCE

Most might instinctively say that property taxes are the reason rural schools spend less than urban and suburban school districts. To an extent, that's true; however, property taxes don't account for all of the disparity. Indeed, if property tax were replaced with a local income tax or a local sales tax, many of the same problems would remain. Nevertheless, most states do utilize the property tax. This section discusses how state policies, such as assessment and tax policies, impact the ability of rural districts to raise more funds locally. It will also discuss other factors, such as how specific aspects of funding formulas may favor urban school districts over rural districts when it comes to state funds.

### Rural Property Is Undervalued and Underassessed

In 2017, the state of Missouri collected more than $7.2 billion in property taxes. This included all local taxes for schools, police, fire, and other local services. Interestingly, just 1.76 percent of the revenue came from agricultural property taxes. This is an incredibly low percentage given the fact that approximately two-thirds of Missouri's 44.7 million acres are considered farmland. In comparison, motor-vehicle taxes accounted for 12.13 percent, commercial for 20.78 percent, and residential for 50.23 percent.[9]

The tremendous disparity stems from the way Missouri assesses and taxes farmland. The Missouri Constitution separates property into three classifications: personal, intangible, and real property. Personal property is described as property that is not affixed to a specific location, such as boats, cars, and farm equipment. Intangible personal property includes stocks, bonds, and the like. Real property includes land, permanent structures, and improvements to the land.

However, not all real property is treated the same. The state separates real property into three subclasses: residential property; agricultural or horticultural property; and utility, industrial, and railroad property. It is here that a great disparity begins to emerge between residential and agricultural assessments.

The methods used to appraise residential and agricultural land are very different. Assessors of residential land may use a market approach or a cost approach to determine the value of a piece of property. In the market approach, the assessor compares a property to the recent sales of similar properties in the area, whereas, when applying the cost approach, the assessor considers how much it would cost to replace the property that is being assessed.

Farmland assessment uses neither of these approaches. Instead, the Missouri Tax Commission assigns a grade of one to eight to farmland based on the quality of the land. Each grade of land is assigned a dollar value for assessment purposes (table 6.1). The best, most-valuable piece of farmland in Missouri is assessed at $1,035 per acre. The lowest-grade farmland is assessed at just $31 per acre. Nearly 50 percent of all farmland is in the lowest three grades.

These practices require Missouri assessors to assess farmland at a rate that is lower than the market value of the property, a practice common throughout the country. Researchers John E. Anderson, Seth H. Giertz, and Shafiun N. Shimul report, "From 1960 to 1995, all 50 states adopted some form of use-value assessment (UVA) for agricultural land. UVA programs treat agricultural land preferentially for property tax purposes, basing valuations only on prospective returns from agricultural activity, even when development opportunities are lucrative or are expected to be so in the future."[10] These practices lead to fewer dollars being collected in rural communities.

Some states go a step farther by offering explicit incentives for landowners to not develop certain parcels of land. Jeffrey Sundberg, a business and economics professor at Lake Forest College, has identified as many as twenty-three states that have such policies.[11] These programs, depending on the design, can greatly impact local school districts by reducing the assessed value of rural property. Sundberg notes that the program in Georgia resulted in nearly an 80 percent reduction in property taxes collected from eligible properties in Georgia.

This is not to say that these programs aren't worthwhile. For example, it could be argued that farmers deserve preferential tax treatment and that, by doing so, states also serve residents in other parts of the state. The point here is that these practices place rural school districts at a disadvantage when attempting to raise funds locally for public education or other public services.

In Missouri, for instance, the U.S. Department of Agriculture calculated the value of Missouri farmland at $96.2 billion in 2016.[12] Missouri's assessment practices, however, value the property at just $10.3 billion. This is an effective assessment rate of less than 11 percent, significantly lower than the 19 percent assessment rate on residential property and 32 percent on commercial.[13]

Figure 6.1 displays the assessed valuation per pupil for different types of school districts. In this figure, the size of the school district was not taken into account. Rather, each school district was treated as a unit of equal size. As such, each bar represents the average for all of the school districts in the category.

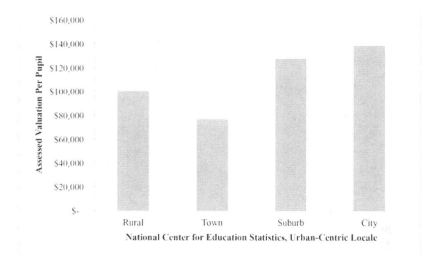

**Figure 6.1 Missouri Assessed Valuation of Property per Pupil by Urban Centric Locale, 2016.** *Source:* **National Center for Education Statistics**

As the figure shows, suburban and city school districts have considerably more local wealth per pupil. City school districts, for instance, have 181 percent of the local property wealth of town school districts. This gap would not be closed if assessment practices were changed, but it would be diminished.

## Some Rural School Districts Tax Themselves Less

With deflated property assessments, rural school districts have tough financial challenges not faced by their suburban and urban counterparts. To overcome this, residents of local school districts would have to tax themselves at a higher rate to generate revenue at similar levels as their peers. Some rural school districts have done this, especially prior to states implementing foundation formulas that take into account local effort. In many cases, however, this isn't the reality. Rather, rural school districts often tax themselves less than their more affluent peers.

Missouri allows local school districts to have a lot of control over their tax rates. The average tax-rate ceiling—that is, the highest voter-approved tax rate for a local school district—in urban school districts is $4.408 per $100 of assessed valuation. Suburban school districts are not far behind at $4.203. The average tax-rate ceiling in rural school districts is $3.637 and just $3.348 in town school districts. Figure 6.2 displays these rates alongside the town and rural rates, which are significantly lower.

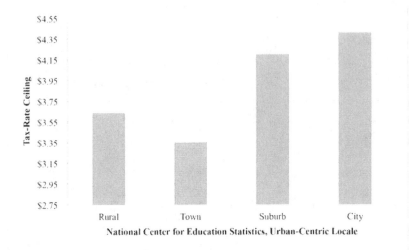

**Figure 6.2   Missouri Average Tax-Rate Ceiling by Urban Centric Locale, 2016.** *Source:* **National Center for Education Statistics**

The difference between town school districts and suburban districts is $0.85. This might seem like a small amount, but it is not. It is a difference of more than 30 percent. To put this into perspective, the average assessed valuation for school districts in Missouri is roughly $182 million. The higher city tax rate would generate $1.93 million more than the average town tax rate, or roughly $1,158 per pupil.

Missouri's foundation formula for state aid to schools takes into account how much school districts can raise locally. It then adjusts the amount of state aid based on this amount. This is a boon for rural schools as it helps level the playing field between property-rich and property-poor school districts. Yet, the formula does not account for different local tax rates.

Currently, the state assumes a local tax rate of $3.43 per $100 of assessed valuation. As such, school districts that tax themselves above this amount do not lose state aid. They simply raise more money, outside the formula. This is a prominent feature of local control and could be considered a desirable feature: It encourages communities to invest more in their schools without the penalty of those funds being diverted to another community.

The most interesting thing is not that some districts choose to tax themselves more than state's formula amount; it is that many districts choose to tax themselves at a rate below the state-assumed rate. In 2016, 216 school districts—more than 40 percent of Missouri school districts—did so, and the districts that did so were not random. In total, 96 percent of those districts were either rural or town school districts.

Amazingly, sixty-four school districts tax themselves at the state-mandated minimum of $2.75 per $100 of assessed valuation. Among these, sixty-two are either rural or town school districts. These districts would not lose state money by taxing themselves at a higher rate. The state-assumed local effort is independent of how much a school district actually raises. Therefore, this low tax rate in these school districts seems to indicate a local preference for lower taxes.

Again, it's important to remember not to paint all rural schools with too broad of a brush. Not all rural and town school districts tax themselves at low rates; some choose higher rates. The ability for local school districts to set their own tax rates nevertheless exacerbates significant disparities in spending among school districts. For instance, among the ten low-spending rural and town school districts, the tax-rate ceiling is just $2.88 per $100 of assessed valuation. In the nine high-spending rural districts referenced earlier, the rate was $4.39 per $100 of assessed valuation—a difference of $1.51. The low-spending districts would not rise to the top if they were to increase their tax rate, but they would decrease the disparity among school districts.

The focus on "local control" allows local school districts to set their own tax rate. Yet, this in and of itself helps to further disparities among school districts. In other words, local control and equity may be in direct conflict with one another. This would be the case even when comparing two school districts with identical property tax wealth. Different tax rates, set by local taxpayers, would result in different amounts of revenue for the school district.

In the case of rural school finance, we are not talking about districts with identical means. As this chapter has seen, rural schools have significantly less property value per pupil. When they also tax themselves less, this creates an even larger gulf between the haves and the have-nots. This brings up an interesting question: Why do they set lower tax rates?

When it comes to the literature on tax levy voting, two clear patterns emerge. First, older people tend to vote more often than younger voters. Second, people with higher levels of education and higher socioeconomic status tend to vote to increase taxes more frequently than their less educated, less affluent peers. These factors do not bode well for rural and small town school districts.

Rural school districts have more senior citizens as a percentage of the total voting population. The U.S. Census reports the median age for adults in rural areas is fifty-one, while it is only forty-five in urban areas.[14] Five-year estimates from the U.S. Census Bureau's American Community Survey note that only 19.5 percent of rural residents age eighteen or older have a bachelor's degree or higher. Meanwhile, 29 percent do so in urban communities. This is a staggering difference.

The end result is that rural communities tend to tax themselves less than their peers in more urbanized areas. Our system, which allows for local control of taxation, allows for some disparities to creep into the system. It allows citizens in areas with more property wealth to choose to tax themselves at higher rates than citizens in areas with less property wealth.

## Funding Formulas Can Favor Urban Districts

The first two factors presented here describe how state and local policies make it difficult for rural school districts to raise funds through property taxes. Some states also expect rural schools to spend less than their counterparts and weight rural students less in funding formulas. This specifically comes into play in states with cost-of-living adjustments.

Clearly, it costs more to live in some places than in others. Midwestern states, for instance, typically have a much lower cost of living than both the east and west coasts. Similarly, dollars are not worth the same amount within each state. According to the Education Law Center, twelve states have cost-of-living adjustments in their funding formulas.[15] These adjustments attempt to address this issue.

Typically, cost-of-living factors in state funding formulas benefit urban and suburban school districts by providing additional financial assistance to students in these districts. It costs more to live in these locations; therefore, it must cost more to educate students, so the logic goes.

While this is probably true—in that competing salaries are higher in urban and suburban areas—cost-of-living adjustments do not consider that rural school districts face particular challenges in recruiting talented individuals to low-paying jobs in outstate areas. Accounting for this fact in state funding formulas would be particularly challenging, especially if you want to do it in a way that doesn't incentivize gaming of the system.

Missouri's school funding formula follows an adequacy model: it attempts to ensure that every school district in the state has an adequate amount of

Table 6.1   Percentage of Missouri Agricultural Land by Agricultural Land Grades

| Land Grade | Assessed Value | % of Agricultural Land |
|---|---|---|
| 1 | $1,035 | 1% |
| 2 | $850 | 3% |
| 3 | $645 | 12% |
| 4 | $405 | 19% |
| 5 | $205 | 17% |
| 6 | $158 | 24% |
| 7 | $79 | 23% |
| 8 | $31 | 1% |

money to provide a quality education. The Foundation Formula multiplies weighted average daily attendance with the State Adequacy Target, the "adequate" dollar amount, and then multiplies that by the Dollar Value Modifier (DVM), the cost-of-living adjustment.[16] The DVM is a ratio calculated using two measures, the regional wage per job and the state median wage per job.

The state does not want to take money away from school districts, but rather provide more to districts where it is expensive for schools to operate. As such, no school district is given a DVM below 1.0, whereas the DVM is above 1.0 for more affluent or expensive areas of the state. The primary beneficiaries of the DVM are suburban and city school districts, where high-paying jobs abound. Indeed, the DVM for St. Louis–area school districts is the highest in the state at 1.092. This results in these districts essentially receiving 9.2 percent more funding from the state than a rural district with a DVM of 1.0.

This is not to suggest that it does not cost more to hire teachers in urban settings or that wages should probably be higher in these areas. Rather, state funding formulas may favor, correctly or incorrectly, some areas of the state over others. The challenge with this type of adjustment to state aid is that these cost-of-living adjustments do not actually take into account the difficulties rural school districts face in attracting high-quality teachers.

Nor do they take into account other school-level factors. Missouri's DVM only relies on measures of wages in the area. This leads urban schools in Missouri to receive more funds than they would absent an adjustment for the cost of living. It does not punish rural schools by reducing funds, and removing the DVM would not increase funds to rural schools. Rather, it would just decrease funds for urban and suburban school districts.

Some states counteract the cost-of-living adjustment or simply award greater funds to rural schools through other formula factors. For instance, twenty-seven states have a "Small District Factor" in their state funding systems.[17] Though this undoubtedly helps rural school districts, it is not the same as accounting for staffing and other difficulties faced by rural schools. To date, no state has been able to do that very well. It may be that the task is impossible or politically infeasible.

Moreover, urban schools could just as easily make a case that they also have difficulties endemic only to urban education. The challenge for state policymakers is to create a formula that fairly recognizes these differences, while also creating a funding system that is not overly complex as to be incomprehensible.

The bottom line in understanding spending differences between rural and urban school districts is clear: When state funding formulas award urban and suburban school districts more in an effort to adjust for cost-of-living differences, they often exacerbate spending differences between city/suburban school districts and town/rural school districts.

## WHAT DOES ALL THIS MEAN FOR RURAL SCHOOLS?

The lack of revenue from local sources for rural schools means rural schools rely more heavily on the state for financial support. In Missouri, suburban and city school districts generate more than 60 percent of PPEs locally. Meanwhile, town and rural school districts generate roughly 45 percent of their revenue locally. This translates to a difference of $1,666 per pupil between rural and suburban school districts and $3,103 between town and city school districts.

In 2016, the average rural and town school districts in the United States received nearly 44 percent of their operating funds from the state. In comparison, suburban school districts received 33 percent and city school districts received just 26 percent. The larger state support for rural and town districts narrows the gap in spending between the types of schools, but does not close it. If, however, rural and town districts chose to tax themselves at commensurate rates as urban school districts, we would expect this gap to narrow further. Figure 6.3 presents the average spending by urban-centric locale and breaks the spending down by federal, state, and local share.

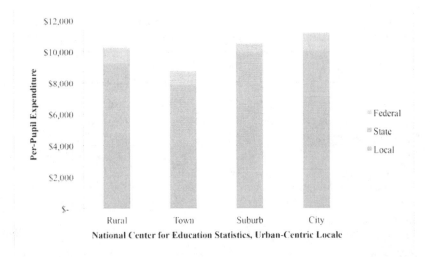

Figure 6.3   Missouri Average Spending by Urban-Centric Locale, 2016. *Source:* National Center for Education Statistics

Hold-harmless provisions may also provide additional assistance for rural school districts. Missouri's small schools with fewer than 350 students, a total of 191 Missouri districts, are held harmless. They are guaranteed a specific level of funding. If the district loses students, they continue to get the same total dollar amount. This can lead to large increases in per-pupil spending, with no change in total spending, as enrollment drops. This process is known to some education scholars as "funding phantom students."[18]

Some states build in a subsidy for small school districts into the funding formula. These formulas often weight students in districts with relatively few students, providing more funds to the school district. Other states award small school districts extra funds outside of the formula. These targeted funds to small or rural school districts are often referred to as "categorical" funds. Categorical funds are often used to fund specific programs and are usually limited in use. Categorical funds for small schools may be used to subsidize salaries, reduce class sizes, or for a variety of other purposes as designated by the legislature or State Department of Education.

One complaint of rural schools relying more heavily on state support is that taxpayers in suburban and urban environments tend to subsidize education in rural areas. State support for education typically comes from a general revenue fund. This is often derived from state income taxes. Taxpayers in the suburbs and cities earn more income; therefore, they typically pay more income taxes. To some, this creates animosity between different areas of the state where some perceive rural communities as not pulling their weight. This situation is exacerbated when urban taxpayers realize they are also paying more in local property taxes than their peers elsewhere.

In Missouri, $15 million is set aside, outside of the funding formula, for school districts with fewer than 350 students. This amount is specified in state statute. While categorical funds, such as these, may go a long way in helping small school districts cope with their financial situation, they also tend to bring more political gamesmanship into the funding process. Unlike school funding formulas, which cover all districts, categorical funds are targeted. This means many lawmakers may not represent school districts that receive the funds. As such, they may see the marked funds as "on the table" when budget discussions arise.

Wisconsin has a categorical fund known as "sparsity aid" for small school districts. These funds are placed into the budget by the governor and then determined by the political process. As lawmakers compete for preferred budget items, it is not uncommon for categorical funds for small schools to be part of that process.

In 2017, for example, Wisconsin governor Scott Walker proposed an $18 million increase in sparsity aid in his budget proposal. Ultimately, the increase was removed by the state's Joint Committee on Finance. According to the committee chair, the committee wanted to look for more long-term solutions to the problems of small school districts, such as sharing adminis-trative functions. These are often some of the same suggestions made by state lawmakers who push for school consolidation.

When the state of Arkansas lost the decade-long Lake View school-finance case, the state was forced to bring the school funding system into compliance with the court's ruling. When the state legislature convened in 2003, they began discussing remedies to the state's funding disparities. As University of Arkansas professor Gary Ritter notes, "Governor [Mike] Huckabee opened with a proposal for far-reaching school consolidation, arguing that this would yield the efficiency necessary to comply with the court's ruling."[19] The debate, as you might imagine in a rural state, was quite contentious.

At the end of the session, the legislature had failed to address the issues laid out by the state's high court and the governor was forced to call a special session. In the end, lawmakers passed a law that contained a slate of reforms, including an increase in base funding for schools, increased base salaries for teachers, increased state sales taxes, and a school-consolidation requirement. Huckabee's original plan would have required school districts with fewer than 1,500 students to consolidate. The final bill agreed to by the legislature lowered that number considerably to 350 students.

Whether attempting to save some money in the state budget or to create a more efficient or equitable system, state lawmakers often look to school consolidation to address the issue. This is a major challenge faced by rural school districts. The cards are stacked so that they are unable to fund them-selves at a level commensurate with their peers, their categorical funding is often in jeopardy, and the school districts themselves are often seen as part of the problem.

Of course, school quality and opportunity is considered as part of the discus-sion around school consolidation; but it must be remembered that the primary impetus for most school and school district closure is finances, not quality.

## CONCLUSION

Rural school finance is a story of contradiction—or, more accurately, of com-peting interests. This, of course, is true for most thorny public-policy issues and for educational issues in more urban centers as well. Nevertheless, the competing interests in urban education rarely threaten the school system's very existence. They do in rural education.

Rural schools find it difficult to fully compete with their peers in other school districts. Rural schools struggle to offer the same number of high-level courses for students. Due to their small size, they lack economies of scale and find it difficult to attract and retain teachers in these subject areas. Moreover, because they lack the ability to fund themselves at levels commensurate with more urbanized districts, they rely more heavily on state aid. This puts a target on the back of rural school districts.

The discussion here should not be taken to suggest school consolidation cannot serve a useful purpose. Indeed, many small, rural school districts (and their students, in particular) may benefit from consolidating with other nearby school districts. Similarly, taxpayers may benefit from consolidating duplicative services or school administrators. Yet, it cannot be ignored that rural communities see these proposals as a threat. They worry that consolidating will force the school to lose its identity. This is a real concern.

Given the gravity of the circumstances, here are four things policymakers need to keep in mind as they look at issues related to rural school finance:

## Don't Simply Look at Per-Pupil Expenditures

When considering how best to support rural school districts and students, lawmakers would be wise to follow this simple guideline: PPEs simply cannot be viewed as a direct measure of school district performance or effectiveness. Doing so claims victory when there is none. For example, if a school district with 100 students that spends $20,000 per student merges into a larger district with 1,000 students and a PPE of $10,000, the new PPE will look very reasonable at just under $11,000 per pupil. Yet, students and the local community will have saved nothing if something else in the district does not change.

The state may save some categorical funds for small schools, depending upon how the aid is determined, but it is not clear what ultimate effect this will have. It makes little sense to consolidate a high-performing rural school district that is sufficiently self-supporting simply to appear to have generated cost savings.

## Understand How State Assessment Practices Impact Rural Schools

There may be a reason that local effort in small, rural schools cannot keep pace with other schools. If the state's tax policy for agricultural land places rural school districts at a disadvantage, then the state might be expected to contribute more to support rural education programs. If states do not build in additional support in their funding formula for rural schools to offset this, they may be encouraging rural schools to set higher tax rates. This can become a recipe for future litigation.

## Recognize the Tension between Equity and Local Control

If local communities are allowed to tax themselves at varying rates, some disparities in PPEs should be expected. These are not the fault of any school district; they are simply the product a system that has competing values. Policymakers and the public must understand and grapple with the competing ideas of equity and local control of education. They must decide, individually and overall, if they can pursue these two views simultaneously, and if so, to what level. They should keep in mind, however, that when calculating measures of equity, how local tax decisions impact the measurement must also be considered.

## Be Aware That School Finance Is Subjective

Too often, issues related to school finance are approached with an empirical eye. One looks at the numbers and tries to show why a school district needs more money, why the state should increase support for education, or why a system is inequitable—as if questions related to adequacy and equity could ever be answered by simply conducting an analysis. Sure, one can calculate how much districts are spending, or look at gaps between districts, or even attempt elaborate schemes to cost-out how much it would cost to provide an adequate education. The truth is, however, that most school-finance decisions boil down to values and the decisions are subjective.

Take, for instance, the case of the small, rural school district with fewer than 100 students. Should that school district be allowed to exist? That is not an empirical question. One can look at the evidence and see if the district is performing on par with other districts. One can look at spending measures and consider efficiencies, but those data points do not tell you whether the school should be consolidated.

Moreover, data cannot tell us whether the state has a duty to subsidize a school district above and beyond what is normal, especially when the district's citizens tax themselves at a relatively low rate. At best, analysis can help us make informed decisions. These are philosophical and political questions. As such, they deserve careful examination and rigorous debate in the public square. At the end of the day, however, it must be recognized that different people will arrive at different conclusions.

## NOTES

1 William S. Koski and Jesse Hahnel, "The Past, Present and Possible Futures of Educational Finance Reform," in *The Handbook of Research in Education*

*Finance and Policy*, eds. Heled F. Ladd and Edward B. Fiske (London: Routledge, 2008), 42–60.

2  Jeffrey S. Sutton, "San Antonio Independent School District v. Rodriguez and Its Aftermath," *Virginia Law Review* 94, no. 8 (December 2008), 1963–86.

3  "School Funding Court Decisions," SchoolFunding.Info, accessed November 14, 2017, http://schoolfunding.info/school-funding-court-decisions/.

4  A. J. Meadows, *The Future of the Universe* (New York: Springer, 2007).

5  National Center for Education Statistics, "Locale Classifications and Criteria," accessed November 14, 2017, https://nces.ed.gov/programs/edge/docs/LOCALE_DEFINITIONS.pdf.

6  James W. Guthrie, "Organizational Scale and School Success," *Educational Evaluation and Policy Analysis* 1, no. 1 (January 1979), 17–27.

7  Matthew Andrews, William Duncombe, and John Yinger, "Revisiting Economies of Size in American Education: Are We Any Closer to a Consensus?," *Economics of Education Review* 21, no. 3 (2002), 245–62.

8  National Center for Education Statistics, "Table E.1.a.-2 Total and Current Expenditures Per Public Elementary and Secondary Student, by District Poverty Level and Urban-Centric 12-Category Locale: 2011–12," Rural Education in America, accessed November 15, 2017, https://nces.ed.gov/surveys/ruraled/tables/E.1.a.-2.asp.

9  Missouri Department of Revenue, "Who Paid the 2016 Property Tax?," accessed November 15, 2017, https://stc.mo.gov/wp-content/uploads/sites/5/2017/04/Who-Paid-Property-Taxes-in-2016-Chart.pdf.

10  John E. Anderson, Seth H. Giertz, and Shafiun N. Shimul, "Property Taxes for Agriculture: Use-Value Assessment and Urbanization across the United States," Mercatus Working Paper, Mercatus Center at George Mason University (August 2015).

11  Jeffrey Sundberg, "Preferential Assessment for Open Space," *Public Finance and Management* 14, no. 2 (2014), 165.

12  U.S. Department of Agriculture, "Land Values: 2017 Summary," last modified August 2017, http://usda.mannlib.cornell.edu/usda/current/AgriLandVa/AgriLandVa-08-03-2017.pdf.

13  Missouri State Tax Commission, "Property Reassessment and Taxation," last modified January 2017, https://stc.mo.gov/wp-content/uploads/sites/5/2017/01/Property-Reassessment-Pamphlet-1-18-16.pdf.

14  U.S. Census Bureau, "New Census Data Show Differences between Urban and Rural Populations," accessed November 15, 2017, https://www.census.gov/newsroom/press-releases/2016/cb16-210.html.

15  Education Law Center, "Funding, Formulas, and Fairness: What Pennsylvania Can Learn from Other States' Education Funding Formulas," last modified February 2013, https://www.elc-pa.org/wp-content/uploads/2013/02/ELC_schoolfundingreport.2013.pdf.

16  James V. Shuls, "A Primer on Missouri's Foundation Formula for K-12 Public Education," Show-Me Institute, Policy Study 40 (March 2017).

17 "Funding, Formulas, and Fairness: What Pennsylvania Can Learn from Other States' Education Funding Formulas," Education Law Center, February 2013, https://www.elc-pa.org/wp-content/uploads/2013/02/ELC_schoolfundingreport.2013.pdf.

18 Jon Fullerton and Marguerite Roza, "Funding Phantom Students," *Education Next* 13, no. 3 (Summer 2013), 9–16.

19 Gary W. Ritter, "Education Reform in Arkansas: Past and Present," in *Reforming Education in Arkansas: Recommendations from the Koret Task Force*, eds. John Brown and Gary Ritter (Stanford, CA: Hoover Institution Press, 2005), 27–42.

*Chapter 7*

# Staffing America's Rural Schools

## Daniel Player and Aliza Husain

In education research, no empirical relationship has been established as consistently and conclusively as the link between teacher quality and student achievement. Research literature confirms that teachers are the most important school-related input that relates to student achievement, and recent research shows that the influence of a high-quality teacher extends well beyond the year-end achievement test and into adulthood in terms of college completion, earnings, and wealth accumulation.[1]

Staffing schools with high-quality teachers is the most promising strategy in K–12 schools to improve outcomes for children, but for a variety of reasons this proposition is much easier on paper than it is in practice for rural schools and districts. This chapter highlights the challenges many rural districts and schools face in the urgent task of filling classrooms with high-quality teachers and provides some examples of promising strategies being employed in some rural areas that could serve as a template for others.

Improving teacher quality presents a particularly daunting challenge to many rural schools. While not universally true, many rural schools report that contextual factors such as demographics, geographic realities, and resource constraints create an uphill recruiting battle for the best teachers. Once recruited, some rural schools also find it difficult to retain teachers.

Recent policies designed to improve teacher quality have also put a new strain on rural schools. Because the identification and development of teacher effectiveness have proven to be a significant challenge for all schools—rural and nonrural—many recent reforms have shifted the onus to schools and districts to improve the overall effectiveness of their teachers through selective management of the teacher workforce. Such policies assume that districts and schools can draw from a deep pool of prospective teachers.

But what works in urban and suburban schools—schools that often have a surplus of available teacher candidates—may be infeasible for rural schools and potentially exacerbate the rural disadvantage. The second section of this chapter highlights a few of the challenges these types of policies present to rural schools and districts. In particular, it includes evidence from the implementation of the School Improvement Grant (SIG) program and Race to the Top (RTT) to suggest that rural schools found it difficult to meet the demands of implementing demand-side teacher policies.

The prognosis is not all doom and gloom for rural schools, however. Rural schools may have some advantages over nonrural schools in terms of working conditions and general teacher satisfaction that give them an edge over nonrural schools. Some creative districts and states have implemented innovative strategies to attract and retain teachers in rural schools. The chapter concludes by highlighting a few of these strategies.

Rural schools vary along a number of dimensions, so it is difficult to characterize the challenges faced by the typical rural school. Some rural schools are located relatively close to urban centers, while others may be located in remote areas many miles from the nearest town. Some are located in economically robust areas, such as resort or recreation areas, while others are located in economically depressed locales that have been decimated by economic evolution. In what follows, the chapter provides a general sense of the challenges and opportunities faced by many rural schools, but recognizes that it may not apply equally to all rural schools.

## ATTRACTING AND RETAINING TEACHERS
## IN RURAL SCHOOLS

There are a number of reasons to predict that it may be difficult to attract teachers to some rural areas due to cultural factors in rural communities and the structure of rural schools. The communities in which rural schools are located are unique and perhaps culturally distinct from what teachers are accustomed to. Rural communities are often isolated from urban centers and may lack many of the amenities available to urban and suburban communities.

For example, they sometimes lack attractive housing options for prospective teachers, which has been identified as one key impediment to attracting teachers to rural settings. Remote rural communities also lack some cultural amenities such as movie theaters, shopping, and entertainment.

The small scale of rural communities might make them less attractive for teachers' families as well. Some married teachers might find rural areas unattractive because they lack job opportunities for teachers' spouses while single teachers might spurn rural areas if they perceive a low probability of finding a partner. For example, a recent report from Oklahoma found that rural schools had a significantly more difficult time attracting men and younger teachers,[2] suggesting that these limitations might be important for rural schools.

One demographic factor that influences the availability of teacher candidates is that rural communities tend to have fewer college-educated adults than nonrural areas. Research has found labor markets for teachers to be quite small, with most teachers working within a relatively short distance of where they attended high school. This potentially puts rural areas at a disadvantage in cultivating a pool of available teacher candidates.

Those who attend college from rural areas might also be less inclined to stay in rural areas after completing their degrees. Among students who were surveyed in a national longitudinal sample, rural students were less likely to express interest in college and were more likely to agree with the statement that it was important for them to get away from the area where they attended high school.[3] Taken together, these facts suggest that rural areas might have significantly less depth to their potential teacher pool.

The structure of rural schools may also make it difficult to attract teacher candidates. Rural schools are often small, meaning teachers have fewer opportunities to collaborate with colleagues and specialize in their field of choice. Remote rural areas also offer fewer opportunities for teachers to access professional development and support from district specialists or university faculty. Some rural areas also have student populations that are geographically dispersed in such a way that it is difficult for parents to be as involved as nonrural parents are in their children's education, which some have argued makes the job less appealing for teachers.

Based on the challenges described earlier, the prevailing opinion is that it is difficult to attract teachers to rural areas. One national survey of rural district superintendents found that low salaries are considered to be the predominant reason rural districts struggle with teacher retention.[4] Rural schools pay less on average than nonrural schools, partly due to lower fiscal capacity to raise tax revenue in rural areas, and national surveys have revealed that rural teachers are more likely than nonrural teachers to say they would be willing to leave teaching if a higher paying job came along.

On the other hand, a different national survey of "policy insiders" and rural superintendents asked each group to identify what they thought were the top three challenges for rural schools. While the policy insiders listed recruiting teachers and retaining teachers as the first and second most pressing challenges, respectively, rural superintendents did not list teacher recruitment or retention among their top three concerns.[5]

Whether this suggests teacher recruitment and retention are not as challenging as perceived or that they are major concerns that happen to be eclipsed by even more pressing concerns remains an open question. For this, evidence from a comprehensive national survey of schools and teachers may provide some insight.

## NATIONAL EVIDENCE ON THE DEMAND
## FOR AND SUPPLY OF RURAL TEACHERS

Rather than speculating about the challenge of attracting and retaining teachers in rural schools, it is instructive to objectively contrast the current situation in rural and nonrural schools. For example, are rural schools more likely to report difficulty filling a vacancy than nonrural schools? And, if there are challenges in recruiting, is there evidence of systematic differences observed in the characteristics of teachers in rural schools versus than those in nonrural schools?

The findings for this analysis are from the last four available waves of the Schools and Staffing Survey (SASS), a nationally representative survey conducted periodically by the National Center for Education Statistics. The data in this section reflect responses from surveys conducted in the 1999–2000, 2003–2004, 2007–2008, and 2011–2012 school years. The surveys collected data from schools on the frequency with which they experienced a vacancy and the difficulty in filling that vacancy. The surveys also collected data on teacher characteristics and experiences.

### Rural Teacher Demand: Teacher Vacancies

Across the four waves of the survey, rural schools were slightly less likely to report having at least one vacancy to fill (74 percent) than were nonrural schools (76 percent), but that could be because rural schools are smaller and have fewer positions to fill generally. In general, rural schools were less likely to report needing to fill a vacancy across most subjects. If a school reported having a vacancy to fill, it was asked to report the level of difficulty associated with filling that vacancy.

Somewhat surprisingly, rural schools were no more likely to report difficulty filling a general elementary education position (4 percent) than were nonrural schools (4 percent); but rural schools were slightly more likely to report having difficulty filling a STEM position (34 percent versus 33 percent) and much more likely to report difficulty filling an ELL position (37 percent versus 29 percent).

The challenge in filling positions is more pronounced in remote rural areas. Remote rural areas report higher overall difficulty filling vacant positions (39 percent with vacancies report difficulty filling at least one position) than nonrural areas (32 percent). They report much higher difficulty filling STEM positions (44 percent versus 33 percent) and ELL positions (43 percent versus 29 percent).

Rural areas are idiosyncratic, and the difficulty in filling vacancies could vary from one region of the country to another. There is some evidence that rural schools in the Midwest and the West face greater difficulty filling positions than their nonrural counterparts in those regions (figure 7.1). The same patterns also hold for ELL positions (figure 7.2) and STEM positions (figure 7.3). The most widespread reported difficulty is among Midwestern schools looking to fill ELL vacancies; nearly half of schools with a vacancy in ELL reported difficulty filling the position.

These findings suggest that there is some regional nuance in the size of the rural disadvantage in filling vacancies, but the majority of schools in most rural areas do not report difficulty filling any teaching positions. Whether this represents widespread difficulty or not is, unfortunately, left to interpretation. Rural schools consistently report a more difficult time filling vacancies, although the magnitudes of the rural/nonrural differences tend to be small.

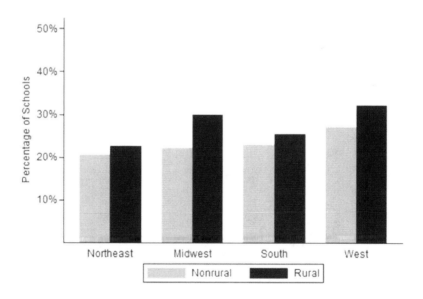

Figure 7.1   Percentage of Schools with at Least One Vacancy That Reported It Was Difficult to Fill a Vacancy, by Rural and Nonrural Status. *Source:* Schools and Staffing Survey, 1999–2012

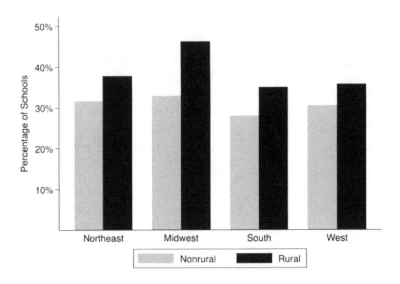

Figure 7.2  Percentage of Schools with an English Language Learner (ELL) Vacancy That Reported It Was Difficult to Fill That Vacancy. *Source:* Schools and Staffing Survey, 1999–2012

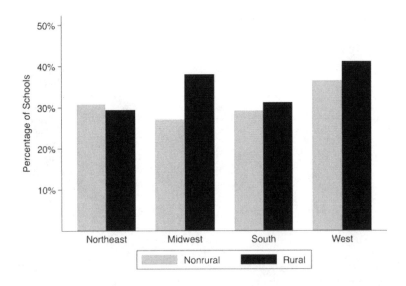

Figure 7.3  Percentage of Schools with a Science, Technology, Engineering, or Math (STEM) Vacancy That Reported It Was Difficult to Fill That Vacancy. *Source:* Schools and Staffing Survey, 1999–2012

The primary concern about teacher vacancies, in terms of teacher effectiveness, is who gets hired to fill those vacancies. That rural schools do not report great difficulty filling vacancies may be a good sign of a healthy pipeline of effective teachers. But, it may be that schools report little difficulty filling positions because they are not as selective with candidates as they should be. A comparison of rural and nonrural teacher characteristics can help with understanding candidates who fill teaching positions.

## Rural Teacher Supply: Characteristics of Teachers in Rural Schools

To what extent does the unique rural setting lead to a different type of teacher being in a rural classroom than a nonrural one? Following are some of the key average trends of teacher characteristics in rural schools and contrast those with nonrural schools.

### Teacher Training

Since 1999–2000, many of the characteristics of teachers in rural schools have been different from those in nonrural schools. For example, teachers in rural areas are less likely than their nonrural counterparts to have graduated from a selective college (14 percent versus 18 percent). This pattern could suggest that teachers in rural areas are less academically prepared than nonrural teachers, or it could simply reflect the fact that well-prepared students from rural areas attend selective colleges at lower rates than nonrural students.

We cannot rule out either mechanism, but the pattern is also consistent with other research that has found lower academic aptitude (measured in terms of test scores) among rural teachers in Kentucky.[6] The disparity is even more pronounced in the most remote rural schools in the United States.

Over the past two decades, there has been an increase in the number of alternative certification programs in which teachers are able to begin teaching without completing a traditional teacher-certification program as part of a bachelor's or master's degree program. While some express concerns about the quality of teachers from alternative certification programs, recent research has largely found them to be as effective as, and sometimes more effective than, traditionally certified teachers in the schools in which they work.[7] In light of emerging evidence, some have held out hope for alternative certification as a way to address the needs of rural schools.

However, as of 2011–2012, there was no evidence of a trend toward alternative certification in rural areas. Overall, teachers from rural areas were less likely to have graduated from an alternative certification program than teachers in urban schools (9 percent versus 13 percent), but there were no meaningful differences between rural teachers and those from suburban schools.

Therefore, it does not appear that rural areas are using alternative certification programs to fill teaching vacancies.

## Advanced Degrees and Experience

Rural teachers are less likely to hold a master's degree than teachers from any other locales despite the fact that they are slightly more experienced, on average, than teachers from urban and suburban settings. In comparison with suburban teachers, for example, rural teachers are more than 20 percent (roughly 10 percentage points) less likely to hold a master's degree. It is not clear what drives these differences.

It could reflect differential access to master's degree programs, differences in the policies of states with relatively fewer or more rural schools, or simply teacher preferences. Whatever the cause, the net result is fewer master's degrees among rural teachers. In light of the lack of evidence connecting master's degrees with teacher effectiveness, this disparity might be less troubling than it first appears.[8]

Teacher experience has been shown to influence teacher effectiveness, and the returns are typically largest in the first several years of teaching.[9] Another useful measure of teacher experience is the percentage of teachers who are in their first three years of teaching. If rural teachers tended to turn over in their first few years, either due to unexpected challenges of working in rural environments or because of programs (e.g., Teach for America) that do not emphasize long-term teaching commitments, one would expect to see a disproportionate number of rural schools being staffed with novice teachers.

However, rural schools have fewer novice teachers than urban schools and more than town schools, and are statistically indistinguishable from suburban schools. Thus, it does not appear that rural schools have a greater reliance on novice teachers than nonrural schools.

## Teacher Demographics

Matches between a teacher's race and her student's race have been shown to have a positive impact on student achievement through a hypothesized mentor effect. Because rural areas have experienced demographic shifts over the past decade, it is worth examining the demographics of the teacher labor force to see how they differ across locales and whether rural students appear to be at a disadvantage in having a teacher of the same race or ethnicity.

On average, rural schools have fewer black and Hispanic teachers than nonrural schools. The difference is most pronounced when compared with urban schools, which hire four times as many black teachers on average. However, this trend could reflect population differences between urban and rural areas. After including a simple control for the percentage of the student body that is minority, rural schools actually employ a statistically *greater* percentage of black and Hispanic teachers than their suburban and town counterparts. This suggests, for example, that a rural area with 20 percent black students tends to have more black teachers than an urban area with 20 percent black students.

In sum, comparing teacher characteristics in rural versus nonrural schools reveals some differences in terms of degree attainment, training, and the selectivity of college from which teachers graduated, although the rural/nonrural differences tend to be fairly small. Without more objective measures of actual quality, one cannot say whether these characteristics portend a difference in classroom effectiveness, but they do suggest there could be some differences between the types of teachers who end up in rural schools compared with those who are teaching in nonrural schools. Further research on the topic is certainly warranted to know the degree to which classroom effectiveness is different for rural versus nonrural teachers.

## TEACHER POLICIES AND THEIR EFFECTS
## ON RURAL SCHOOLS

The data on teacher vacancies and teacher characteristics are, unfortunately, somewhat dated because they do not span the course of the most recent wave of federal and state reforms that have focused most intensely on teacher quality. Due to the challenge inherent in identifying teacher quality, some of these policies have been designed in ways that might actually have a negative impact on teacher quality in rural areas. While that hypothesis cannot be explicitly tested, following are some recent policies and how they could impact rural schools.

### Measuring Teacher Quality

Teacher quality is difficult to measure and even more difficult to predict. Research has failed to find a consistent link between teacher effectiveness and easily observed teacher attributes such as whether the teacher holds a master's degree and her college major.[10] Therefore, when districts and schools hire new teachers, particularly those right out of education training programs, they are often rolling the proverbial dice. Indeed, the task of hiring a high-quality teacher has been compared to the challenge of predicting NFL quarterback success based on college performance, a notoriously difficult task.[11]

Given the challenges of predicting teacher quality, how do we know with such certainty that teacher effectiveness makes a difference in student achievement? What we know about teacher quality comes from post-hoc measures of "value-added," or the degree to which teachers increased student achievement over the course of the year in which they taught them.

Studies that have used these measures have shown conclusively that there are real differences in teacher quality, and that teacher quality persists from one year to the next; a teacher with high value-added in one year is more likely than other teachers to have high value-added in subsequent years. For example, a very influential recent paper showed that high value-added teachers have lasting influence on student outcomes, even into adulthood.[12] Increasingly, states and districts have begun to use these measures to make policy around teacher quality.

An obvious disadvantage of post-hoc measures of teacher effectiveness is that they can only be measured after the teacher has been in the class-room, and typically only after the first few years of a teacher's career.[13] Districts wishing to identify effective teachers must wait until teacher quality is revealed and then make personnel decisions accordingly. Many recent teacher-quality improvement policies reflect this limitation by focusing on the districts and schools, or on the demand side of the teacher labor market, rather than teacher-preparation programs and professional-development providers, or the supply side of the teacher-quality market.

## The Implementation of Demand-Side Approaches

Since districts cannot easily make informed decisions beforehand about who will be most effective, some districts, such as District of Columbia Public Schools (DCPS), have implemented teacher-evaluation and -accountability programs that identify the lowest-performing teachers and, based on their performance level, offer either a probationary remediation period or sever their contracts altogether. Such accountability systems reduce the likelihood that an ineffective teacher remains in the system indefinitely.

Federal programs such as RTT have spurred some states to adopt similar accountability systems aimed at identifying and rewarding highly effective teachers and removing the least-effective teachers from the public-school system. Although evidence of the actual efficacy of these programs has not been conclusively established, there is some evidence that these types of policies have had an overall positive effect on average teacher quality in some urban school districts where they have been implemented. No conclusive evidence exists for rural districts.

A second example of a policy designed to replace ineffective teachers is the SIG program, in which federal dollars are awarded to states to allocate to districts to improve their lowest-performing schools. With these grants, schools targeted for turnaround were required to replace at least 50 percent of their staff. The theory behind this model of school improvement was that schools would identify the teachers who were least effective and replace them with better-performing teachers.

The federal guidance on SIG did not specify how districts were to identify their least-effective teachers, only that they should be consistent with "locally adopted competencies." The presumption was that districts would have the capacity to release those who struggled most and hire, as replacements, more effective teachers. As with teacher-accountability policies, the assumption behind this type of mandate is that schools would be able to go to a deep pool of teacher candidates to replace the dismissed teachers with more effective ones.

Is there a sufficient teacher supply to support demand-side approaches to improve teacher effectiveness? Almost certainly, the answer to this question is that it depends. The best evidence suggests that the United States does not currently have a universal teacher-supply problem; teacher-preparation programs graduate about twice as many potential teachers as there are teaching vacancies each year.[14]

Although a universal shortage does not exist, the data presented earlier in the chapter illustrate that not all teaching positions are equally easy to fill; shortages almost certainly exist in particular subject areas and locales. The prospect of effectively addressing teacher quality through demand-side policies is likely to be more tenable in areas with a deeper potential-teacher pool from which to select new teachers, and those areas are less likely to be in rural areas. If rural districts were to eliminate their least-effective teachers, how realistic is it that they would be able to hire more-effective teachers to take their place?

Emerging evidence from the implementation of demand-side approaches to improving teacher quality suggests that rural schools have struggled to implement these policies as designed. For example, SIG was designed to provide some flexibility as schools targeted for improvement could choose one of four models: Transformation, Turnaround, Restart, or Closure.

For many rural schools, Turnaround, Restart, and Closure were not feasible options because they required either replacement of 50 percent of staff (Turnaround), access to a charter management organization (Restart), or reasonable student access to other schools that would be required with a school closure. As one might suspect, Transformation was the most common choice for all schools nationwide, but rural schools that were targeted for improvement were much more likely than nonrural improvement schools to select the Transformation model.

A case study of rural SIG schools conducted by Mathematica Policy Research sheds some light on implementation challenges that are unique to the rural context.[15] The schools in their sample reported that recruiting and retaining teachers was difficult because the schools were located far from the district's larger population center, which teachers found unappealing. The schools also perceived that their isolation from university programs and the amenities common to nonrural areas made it more difficult to access qualified teacher-applicant pools.

In total, eight of the nine schools studied listed recruiting and retaining teachers as a key challenge in implementing SIG as it had been designed. Schools also noted that it was difficult to comply with other improvement strategies, such as increasing learning time, because of transportation costs and constraints.

While the evidence on the effectiveness of demand-side teacher-quality policies in rural areas is still uncertain, it is clear that the trend is moving toward a greater reliance on a robust teacher-applicant pool. There is good reason to believe that this is a tall order for many rural schools, so greater emphasis should be given to strategies to attract and retain teachers in rural areas.

## STRATEGIES TO ATTRACT AND RETAIN TEACHERS

Not all is negative when it comes to rural teacher labor markets. For instance, rural teachers in the United States are more likely than nonrural teachers to strongly agree with the statement that their school is well run and with the statement that they are generally satisfied with their job and that they believe others to be satisfied.[16] In fact, on measures of satisfaction, the only area in which rural teachers report lower satisfaction than their peers is in regards to their satisfaction with their salary.

In general, rural schools have a marketing problem because these are not widely understood facts. There is great promise that rural schools will be able to continue to attract high-quality teachers if they address some of the key challenges of being a teacher in a rural area. Below are four strategies rural schools are using to attract and retain teachers. Unfortunately, the field lacks any real evidence on the effectiveness of these programs to date. However, these are promising strategies that are being implemented to try to improve the situation for rural schools.

### Financial Inducements

One of the most intuitive strategies to attract highly effective teachers to rural areas is to raise the relative salaries in some hard-to-staff rural schools. As described earlier, rural districts pay significantly less than nonrural districts, and rural teachers are less likely to indicate being satisfied with their salaries than are other teachers. Prior research has found a positive connection between teacher salaries and teacher retention.[17]

Thus, salaries could be a sticking point among rural teachers. While it may be difficult to change salary levels across the board, districts can use bonuses, such as signing bonuses or shortage field bonuses, to attract teachers to specific hard-to-staff positions.

The prevalence of these types of bonuses is low overall, and lower in rural areas than nonrural areas. As of the 2011–2012 school year, shortage pay was less than half as common in rural districts (9.9 percent) as it was in urban districts (20 percent).[18] The same pattern follows for student loan forgiveness programs. One innovative strategy that some have implemented is to provide housing vouchers or even subsidized housing to rural teachers. For example, Mississippi passed the Mississippi Critical Teacher Shortage Act of 1998, which provides housing grants of up to $6,000 to cover moving costs, closing costs, and down payments for teachers who commit to teaching in designated high-shortage areas, many of which are in rural areas. Likewise, Minnesota offers student teaching stipends and student loan forgiveness to people who commit to teach in a high-needs area, including rural areas.

## Grow Your Own

Another way to increase the pool of potential teacher candidates is through "grow-your-own" approaches for rural districts. Such programs could either target mid-career alternative teacher candidates or high school students who show an aptitude for teaching. Many such programs have been initiated to address general teacher shortages, but there is little information about how effective they have been at meeting the needs of rural schools. While this is an important unfilled need for future research, following are a few examples of grow-your-own approaches that have been attempted and have the potential to meet the needs of rural schools.

### *Paraprofessional Development Programs*

Paraprofessional educators in rural schools are often from the local community and therefore are less likely to leave rural areas. Programs such as the Pathways to Teaching Careers at Armstrong Atlantic State University in Georgia are an example of a partnership between a school district and a teacher-training program to help develop paraprofessional teachers into full-time classroom teachers.

### *Enhanced Training Opportunities*

Wyoming supports "professional development schools" as training grounds for preservice teachers and recent graduates. This incubator approach allows prospective teachers to get an intense professional-development onboarding experience. Through programs like this, prospective rural teachers could receive practical experience while being supported by peers who understand the demands of teaching in rural settings.

## Preparing Middle and High School Students

Phi Delta Kappa sponsors Future Educators of America (FEA), a program designed to prepare adolescents for careers in education. While there are no examples of rural districts partnering directly with FEA to help prepare students, an evaluation of the FEA program in Georgia found that 20 percent of involved students expressed a desire to one day teach in rural schools.[19] Another example of such a program is Call Me MISTER program through Clemson University that is designed to give high school graduates from underserved communities support to study to become a teacher through one of the participating partner universities.

A third example is the Teacher Cadet Program, which targets talented high school students to consider a career in teaching by providing hands-on experience with education while still in high school. While none are specific to rural contexts, implementing these types of programs in rural schools could strengthen the pipeline of teacher candidates who are committed to serving rural areas.

## Creative Induction

As the least densely populated state in the country, Alaska faces a rural school challenge that is more intense than perhaps any other state. A recent study of some of Alaska's recruitment and retention efforts yields some interesting possibilities for other rural states to consider.[20] Alaska responded to No Child Left Behind by instituting the Alaska Statewide Mentoring Project (ASMP). Recognizing the limited supply of potential mentors in the small, rural schools where new teachers were being hired, this initiative connects experienced full-time mentor teachers throughout the state to beginning teachers through distance technology.

Beginning teachers communicate at least weekly with their mentors over the telephone or computer and mentors visit the class of the new teacher at least once per month to observe classroom instruction and provide feedback. As of 2015, the ASMP served roughly 500 teachers per year. In the six years between 2009 and 2015, the retention rates of new teachers in rural districts increased 10 percentage points, from 67 percent to 77 percent.

## Job Modifications

The growth of technology in rural areas gives rural schools an opportunity to think outside the bounds of the traditional model of a physical teacher in every classroom. Job-sharing programs, in which a consortium of rural schools might share a "virtual" teacher for several periods a day, illustrate how rural schools might begin to think differently about education. In the 2011 SASS, 63 percent of rural schools reported having at least one "distance" class where instruction was delivered to students remotely.

Using distance education in innovative ways is just one example of how rural schools could begin to think about filling hard-to-fill positions. An example of this is the Glenns Ferry (Idaho) School District, which relies on teachers from the Idaho Digital Learning Academy to teach foreign language classes and some AP courses.

## CONCLUSION

Rural schools have more difficulty filling some teaching positions than nonrural schools, but overall, they do not report strikingly different vacancy rates than other nonrural schools. As there is a more intense move toward education policy that is intended to improve teacher quality through hiring the right teachers and dismissing the less effective teachers, rural schools may struggle to keep up because they do not have the same depth in their potential teacher pool that suburban or urban locales might.

National survey responses suggest that teachers in rural schools view their jobs more favorably on average than others, so there is hope that rural schools will continue to be able to compete for the best and brightest. Some innovative strategies are emerging in rural areas that may yield promise for rural schools to attract teachers. Rural schools are as different from one another as any other class of school, though, so schools and districts should work together to develop strategies to address their unique challenges.

## NOTES

1   Note: None of the available research on teacher effectiveness has focused exclusively on rural areas or explored whether there are differences in the effect of teacher quality between rural and nonrural settings. For example, Chetty et al. (2014) was conducted in a large urban district. While there may not be compelling theoretical reasons to believe that the relationship between students and their teachers would be qualitatively different in rural areas, it is a gap in the literature that merits further investigation; see Raj Chetty et al., "Measuring the Impacts of Teachers II," *American Economic Review* 104, no. 9 (September 2014), 2633–29.

2   Valeriy Lazarev, "Indicators of Successful Teacher Recruitment and Retention in Oklahoma Rural School Districts," Institute of Education Sciences, National

Center for Education Evaluation and Regional Assistance, October 2017, https://ies.ed.gov/ncee/edlabs/regions/southwest/pdf/REL_2018275.pdf.

3  Daniel Player, "Take Me Home Country Roads? Exploring the College Attendance Patterns of Rural Youth," Rural Opportunities Consortium of Idaho, July 2015, http://www.rociidaho.org/wp-content/uploads/2015/07/ROCI_Rural-College-Patterns_Final.pdf.

4  Terri Duggan Schwartzbeck et al., "How Are Rural Districts Meeting the Teacher Quality Requirements of No Child Left Behind?," American Association of School Administrators, December 19, 2003, http://aasa.org/uploadedFiles/Policy_and_Advocacy/files/RuralTeacherQualityStudy.pdf.

5  Lars Johnson, Ashley LiBetti, and Andrew Rotherham, "Federal Education Policy in Rural America," Rural Opportunities Consortium of Idaho, December 2014, http://www.rociidaho.org/wp-content/uploads/2015/01/ROCI_2014FedEdPolicy_FINAL_0115.pdf.

6  Jacob Fowles, J. S. Butler, Joshua M. Cowen, Megan E. Streams, and Eugenia F. Toma, "Public Employee Quality in a Geographic Context: A Study of Rural Teachers," *American Review of Public Administration* 44, no. 5 (January 2013), 503–21, https://doi.org/10.1177/0275074012474714.

7  Donald J. Boyd et al., "Teacher Preparation and Student Achievement," *Educational Evaluation and Policy Analysis* 31, no. 4 (December 2009), 416–40, https://doi.org/10.3102/0162373709353129; Jill Constantine et al., "An Evaluation of Teachers Trained through Different Routes to Certification," U.S. Department of Education, Institute of Education Sciences, National Center for Education Evaluation and Regional Assistance, February 2009, https://ies.ed.gov/ncee/pubs/20094043/pdf/20094043.pdf; and Tim Sass, "Certification Requirements and Teacher Quality: A Comparison of Alternative Routes to Teaching" (working paper, National Center for Analysis of Longitudinal Data in Education Research, December 2011), https://caldercenter.org/sites/default/files/Sass_Certification-Requirements.pdf.

8  Matthew M. Chingos and Paul E. Peterson, "It's Easier to Pick a Good Teacher Than to Train One: Familiar and New Results on the Correlates of Teacher Effectiveness," *Economics of Education Review* 30, no. 3 (June 2011), 449–65, https://doi.org/10.1016/j.econedurev.2010.12.010.

9  Dale Ballou and Michael Podgursky, "Returns to Seniority among Public School Teachers," *Journal of Human Resources* 37, no. 4 (Autumn 2002), 892–912, https://doi.org/10.2307/3069620; and Helen F. Ladd and Lucy C. Sorensen, "Returns to Teacher Experience: Student Achievement and Motivation in Middle School," *Education Finance and Policy* 12, no. 2 (April 2016), 241–79, https://doi.org/10.1162/EDFP_a_00194.

10  Chingos and Peterson, "It's Easier to Pick a Good Teacher."

11  Malcolm Gladwell, "Most Likely to Succeed," *New Yorker*, December 8, 2008, https://www.newyorker.com/magazine/2008/12/15/most-likely-to-succeed-malcolm-gladwell.

12  Chetty et al., "Measuring the Impacts of Teachers II."

13  Note: Teacher quality as measured by value-added tends to grow over the course of the first three to four years in the profession. Therefore, the first few years of

teaching might give little information about who will eventually be a successful teacher.

14 James Cowan, Dan Goldhaber, Kyle Hayes, and Roddy Theobald, "Missing Elements in the Discussion of Teacher Shortages," *Educational Researcher* 45, no. 8 (November 2016), 460–62, https://doi.org/10.3102/0013189X16679145.

15 Linda Rosenberg, Megan Davis Christianson, and Megan Hague Angus, "Improvement Efforts in Rural Schools: Experiences of Nine Schools Receiving School Improvement Grants," *Peabody Journal of Education* 90, no. 2 (March 15, 2015), 194–210, https://doi.org/10.1080/0161956X.2015.1022109.

16 Player, *Supply and Demand for Rural Teachers*.

17 Cassandra M. Guarino, Lucrecia Santibanez, and Glenn A. Daley, "Teacher Recruitment and Retention: A Review of the Recent Empirical Literature," *Review of Educational Research* 76, no. 2 (2006), 173–208; Eric A. Hanushek, John F. Kain, and Steven G. Rivkin, "Why Public Schools Lose Teachers," *Journal of Human Resources* 39, no. 2 (2004), 326–54; and Michael Podgursky, Ryan Monroe, and Donald Watson, "The Academic Quality of Public School Teachers: An Analysis of Entry and Exit Behavior," *Economics of Education Review* 23, no. 5 (2004): 507–18.

18 National Center for Education Statistics, "Schools and Staffing Survey, 2011–12," accessed December 7, 2017, https://nces.ed.gov/surveys/sass/question1112.asp.

19 Peter B. Swanson, "Georgia's Grow-Your-Own Teacher Programs Attract the Right Stuff," *High School Journal* 94, no. 3 (May 2011), 119–33, https://doi.org/10.1353/hsj.2011.0006.

20 Barbara L. Adams and Ashley Woods, "A Model for Recruiting and Retaining Teachers in Alaska's Rural K-12 Schools," *Peabody Journal of Education* 90, no. 2 (March 2015), 250–62, https://doi.org/10.1080/0161956X.2015.1022115.

*Chapter 8*

# Right Place, Right Time: The Potential of Rural Charter Schools

## Juliet Squire

Charter schools are a predominantly urban strategy for increasing educational opportunity. There were nearly 4,000 urban charter schools across the country during the 2014–2015 school year, representing more than half of all charters nationwide.[1] On average, urban charter schools demonstrate a positive impact on student outcomes,[2] and some studies suggest they also have a positive influence on the district schools in their vicinity.[3]

Yet for all the growth and promise of charter schools in urban areas, they have relatively little penetration into rural communities. During the 2014–2015 school year, about 10 percent of urban students attended charter schools, compared to 2 percent of rural students.[4]

There are numerous reasons why charter schools have not gained much traction in rural communities. Some barriers and objections to rural charter schools are political, some operational. Some are valid and should induce policymakers and practitioners to be cautious. Others are based on flawed assumptions or a limited view of the chartering mechanism. As the national spotlight shines on the intractable challenges in many rural communities, however, it is worth evaluating all the tools at our disposal and assessing whether and how they might be helpful. One of those tools is charter schooling.

The following analysis assesses whether and how charter schools may be a useful strategy for improving rural education. First, this chapter discusses the barriers and objections to rural charter schools. Then, some ways in which charter schools can help sustain and revive rural communities are explored. Finally, some recommendations are offered for how policymakers and other sector leaders can enable and support rural charter schools—in the right place, at the right time.

## BARRIERS AND OBJECTIONS TO RURAL
## CHARTER SCHOOLS

As of the 2014–2015 school year, there were 769 rural charter schools across the country.[5] There are at least three reasons for the relatively limited number of rural charter schools:

- The operational challenges of opening and operating a charter school in rural areas with small populations and low population density;
- A lack of knowledge of and exposure to charter schools among rural populations; and
- Limited support and strong opposition to rural charter schools among state policymakers.

In considering the potential of rural charter schools, perhaps the most immediately apparent challenges are operational: limited access to start-up funds, tougher economies of scale, and small talent pools for teachers and leaders in geographically isolated communities.

In urban areas, charter growth has relied extensively on start-up funds from federal and philanthropic grants. These funds are essential to support the work that charter-school founders must complete before a charter school opens its doors—from curriculum design and selection, to identifying a facility, to hiring teachers. But these funds have been less readily accessible to rural charter-school founders. The federal Charter Schools Program, which has funneled about $3.4 billion in start-up grants to charter leaders since 1995, only created a priority for rural charter schools in 2010.[6] Meanwhile, most private sources of start-up charter funds have concentrated their support in urban areas.[7]

Financial constraints continue to be an issue for rural charter schools after they open. It is difficult to leverage economies of scale in small rural schools, which typically have higher overhead costs and lower student-to-teacher ratios (i.e., a rural school will need a first-grade teacher whether it enrolls five or twenty-five first graders). Financial viability is already a challenge for traditional-district rural schools.

State funding formulas vary in how they account for limited economies of scale in rural areas, with some providing small districts with as much as 28 percent *more* per pupil (California) and others providing 4 percent *less* per pupil (New York).[8] State funding formulas also vary in how they fund charter schools, but, on average, they receive 72 cents for every per-pupil dollar that district schools receive.[9] State funding formulas hardly make up the difference in the best of circumstances. The constrained budgets of rural schools, combined with lower funding levels for charters, make it more difficult for rural charter schools to break even.

The challenges of economies of scale and financial viability also make it difficult for rural communities to attract charter-management organizations (CMOs). CMOs drive a lot of the charter sector's growth but often prefer to expand to new regions in clusters. That is, expanding CMOs often look for communities that are large enough to sustain five or seven schools. This approach not only allows CMOs to benefit from the economies of scale and collaboration that geographic proximity provides, but also makes them less likely to expand into rural communities.

Finally, rural schools across the country also struggle to recruit and retain high-quality teachers, and it's easy to imagine why this might be just as hard, if not harder, for charters. Rural schools often offer teachers and leaders lower salaries than suburban or even urban schools.[10] Moreover, in small towns, there simply is not the volume of potential hires from whom to select teachers, meaning rural charters may need to recruit educators from the existing system or from outside the community. Both options have obvious drawbacks.

The operational challenges to rural charter schools are significant. However, before rural charter schools can contemplate these operational challenges, they must first address other major obstacles: the lack of knowledge and familiarity with charter schools among rural populations and political environments in which they often have few champions and many opponents.

Among the general public, there remain significant misconceptions about what charter schools are and how they function. Are charter schools public or private? (Public.) Do they charge tuition? (No.) Can any student enroll? (Usually.)

The information gap on charter schools is even more pronounced in rural areas, where policymakers and their constituencies have limited exposure to them. For instance, in a series of focus groups with community members across rural Oklahoma, a prompt about charter schools was most often met with quizzical countenances and uncertainty about their definition.[11] Given the small number of rural charter schools, it's unsurprising that few rural stakeholders have been exposed to them or their potential.

In addition, when it comes to state education politics, rural charter schools have few proponents, but many opponents. Most charter advocates are focused on urban communities, where their work is far from finished. For all of the positive impact of urban charter schools, there is still significant work to be done to increase consistency of outcomes and ensure they lead to long-term student success. There is also still significant opportunity to start new schools and scale existing models within the urban context. In short, urban charter-school supporters have plenty of challenges and opportunities within their existing bailiwick and limited attention to divert to a new and different market.

Advocates who *are* focused on rural charter schools face a very different political dynamic from their urban allies. In urban environments, charter schools have benefited from a bipartisan alliance.

From the political right, free-market Republicans believe that charter schools create a market-like mechanism in public education, in which competition for students fuels system-wide improvement. From the political left, a significant subset of moderate Democrats argue that low-income communities of color should not be confined to persistently low-performing district schools and should enjoy the same school choice often exercised by the affluent.

These arguments fail to establish a meaningful coalition in rural environments, however. Many rural communities are too small to sustain multiple school options; with the notable exception of the rural South and Southwest, most rural communities are Republican and white, offering a limited constituency for Democratic policymakers.

Republican policymakers may be the most likely advocates for rural charter schools, but their support is hardly universal. In the 2017 Education Next–PEPG survey, 30 percent of Republicans were somewhat or strongly opposed to charter schools (48 percent were supportive and 22 percent were neutral).[12] While the survey data are not available by geographic locale, it stands to reason that Republicans who represent communities with limited capacity to support multiple options are less responsive to arguments about choice and competition.

It seems likely that Republican opposition to charter schools is concentrated in rural areas. In fact, charter laws in numerous Republican-controlled states with significant rural populations have special restrictions against rural charter schools—suggesting that charter advocates and policymakers have traded the possibility of rural charter schools to secure charter expansion in urban areas.[13]

Rural charter schools may lack proponents, but they don't lack opponents. Common objections to urban charter schools are even more powerful in the rural context. Does the increasing market share of charter schools drain resources from urban districts? A single charter school of 400 students might attract 1 percent of an urban district's students and 25 percent of a rural district's students. Should communities be wary of outsiders coming into their community and making promises about a new solution to their challenges?

Rural communities can be just as tight-knit as urban communities and skeptical of those who are not familiar with their history and way of life. Do charter schools undermine historical and familial attachment to local schools? Rural schools are often the heartbeat of a community, a unifying entity in small and/or far-flung populations. They engender strong loyalties from community members.

These arguments in opposition to rural charter schools have a grain or more of truth. They are ready-made, resonate with rural audiences, and are rarely effectively countered. It is little surprise, then, with limited political support and the usual opposition, that rural charter schools remain rather rare.

Despite the political and operational challenges to rural charter schools, more than 700 rural charter schools *do exist.*[14] Mixed impacts on student outcomes suggest what we already know: Rural charter schools are not a panacea.[15] But, in the right place and at the right time, rural charter schools can provide valuable benefits.

## BUT STILL . . . THERE'S POTENTIAL

Given the political and operational challenges to rural charter schools, and in light of their mixed track record of success in states where their outcomes have been studied, it is important to be perfectly clear: charter schools cannot and will not *solve* the challenges in rural education. But neither should policymakers and practitioners rule them out as an option. There are at least four ways in which charter schools can help address the challenges in rural education:

- A classic application of chartering: to induce improvement in and provide alternatives to beleaguered district schools;
- Chartering as a mechanism for local control: to create community ownership of school governance and design;
- Charter conversion: using the chartering mechanism to increase autonomy and reduce the burden of compliance and reporting; and
- To meet the needs of specific student populations: Charter schools can often specialize in ways that district schools cannot.

Each opportunity for rural charter schools is discussed in turn later in this chapter.

### A Classic Application of Chartering: To Induce Improvement in and Provide Alternatives to Beleaguered District Schools

Rural schools too often show similar or worse outcomes to their urban counterparts. In addition to middling results on the National Assessment of Educational Progress, rural students are also less likely to take college-preparatory coursework,[19] enroll in AP or IB courses,[20] and enroll in four-year colleges.[21] Those who do enroll in college are less likely to persist to their second year.[22]

In rural communities that are struggling to prepare their students for post-secondary success and are large enough to support more than a single K–12 pathway, rural charter schools can play a role similar to their role in cities: providing alternatives to district schools.

This is the context in which Oklahoma's Academy of Seminole origi- nated.[23] Seminole, Oklahoma, is a small town about sixty miles east southeast of Oklahoma City. The district serves approximately 1,700 students, 59 per- cent of whom are eligible for free or reduced-price lunch.[24] The Seminole

---

## BOX 8.1 A NOTE ON VIRTUAL CHARTER SCHOOLS

This paper focuses on brick-and-mortar rural charter schools, but vir- tual charter schools serve thousands of students in hard-to-reach places. There are 135 full-time virtual charter schools in the United States, serving 180,000 students.[16] At first blush, online options for rural stu- dents may seem like an obvious way to provide options in communities defined by low population density and geographic isolation. But they are not always so easy to access and, even when they are, they often do not provide high-quality instruction.

By virtue of delivering instruction over the Internet, virtual charter schools rely on students' ability to access the Internet. Unfortunately, access to broadband Internet continues to be a challenge in many rural areas. In 2016, the Federal Communications Commission determined that nearly four in ten rural residents lack access to high-speed Internet (defined as 25 megabytes per second). By comparison, just 4 percent of urban residents lack access.[17] While most schools have access to high-speed Internet—and many rural-district students can and do access individual courses through their school's Internet—connectivity in the home continues to be a barrier for rural students to access full-time virtual schools.

Even when rural students have the Internet connectivity necessary to access full-time virtual schools, there are significant questions about instructional quality. In 2015, the Center for Research on Educational Outcomes (CREDO) at Stanford University compared the performance of students in virtual charter schools to students with similar character- istics in traditional public schools. They found that students in virtual charter schools demonstrated 72 fewer days of learning in reading and 180 fewer days of learning in math.[18] Given the challenges in access and quality, there is significant work to be done before full-time virtual schools can reliably provide rural students with greater educational choice and opportunity.

district has four schools, each of which receives a grade between a C and a B- on the state's A–F accountability ratings.[25]

Paul Campbell is the CEO of a local aerospace manufacturing company, EnviroSystems, and is working with local community leaders in Seminole to open a charter school. Campbell's personal story tracks with what he is hoping to create for young people in Seminole. He grew up in rural Kentucky, where his dad was a coal miner. When his family went bankrupt, they left rural Kentucky and moved to the city, where Campbell had access to a school that "changed the trajectory" of his life. Reflecting on his fate compared to those of his childhood peers in rural Kentucky (one died from drug abuse, two are coal miners, and one is in prison for selling methamphetamine), he says, "I wasn't smarter than these guys. It was the opportunity I had through education."

When he took the helm of EnviroSystems a few years ago, his initial assessment of the company and its ability to grow raised significant workforce challenges. To find the skilled labor the company would need, he determined that he either had to move the whole company to a different community, split the company in two and locate the skilled jobs closer to the city, or build and recruit the workforce he needed in Seminole. But, as he stated simply, "Trying to recruit to a town with a poor school is hard."

Knowing that a high-quality school was essential to training and attracting a skilled workforce, Campbell decided to found a nonprofit organization called Advance Rural Education, which is investing in efforts to improve the school district while also starting a STEM charter school.

Campbell's relationship with the district has not always been collaborative. While Campbell has provided financial support to the district for professional development, updating the curriculum, and creating a career pathways program, the district twice rejected his application to open a charter school. In January 2017, the Academy of Seminole finally received a charter after appealing to the Oklahoma State Board of Education. It will open its doors in August 2018.[26]

Asked how his school will affect the local district, Campbell acknowledges that district officials have expressed concerns that his school will make theirs unviable. Others are worried: "What about the kids who are left behind?" Campbell hopes that his parallel investments in improving the district schools will help assuage those concerns but isn't backing off from the charter school approach. "We have to create the reality to demonstrate what's possible," Campbell says. "And then the local schools may start to feed off what we do."

Despite many people's assumptions about the size and structure of rural school systems, there are rural districts that are large enough to support charter schools alongside the district system. In 2014–2015, there were 8,080 rural districts in the United States. Twenty percent offer more than one school option at each grade level, 31 percent had more than 500 students in grades one to eight, and 17 percent had more than 500 students in grades nine to twelve.[27] In these communities, a charter school could provide an alternative to and compete with existing schools.

## Chartering as a Mechanism for Local Control: To Create Community Ownership of School Design and Governance

By virtue of their size and isolation, rural schools face specific challenges regarding school consolidation and governance from afar. Several communities have successfully used the charter mechanism to assert local control over their school and maintain it against impending consolidation.

Terry Ryan, CEO of Bluum, has highlighted Crestone Charter School in Colorado, which parents founded in 1996 after the local school was slated for closure. Parents did not want their children to take long bus rides through wintry weather to a nearby town with mediocre schools, and petitioned for permission to open and operate a charter school.[28] Today, Crestone Charter School serves 97 students in grades K–12, about two-thirds of whom qualify for free or reduced-price lunch, and has exceeded the state's average growth rate on annual assessments.[29]

A similar story has played out in Graysville, Indiana, when the local district school, under threat of consolidation, converted to a charter in 2004.[30] Rural Community Academy's enrollment has increased from 123 students in 2006–2007 to 168 students in 2016–2017 and draws heavily on community partnerships for support and place-based educational opportunities.[31]

In Crestone, Colorado, and Graysville, Indiana, rural communities have founded charter schools as a way to maintain a local school and shape it to community needs and values. These schools have been able to thrive and even helped attract new families to their communities.

The threats of consolidation, which prompted the communities in Crestone and Graysville to found local charter schools, are not uncommon. As their populations continue to dwindle, rural districts and schools receive less funding and find it increasingly difficult to balance budgets. This helped propel the tremendous consolidation that the United States has already witnessed.

In 1920, there were 271,000 schools across the United States serving 24 million students. In 2008, there were less than half as many schools serving twice as many students.[32] School consolidation is still a real possibility for many rural communities, which causes palpable anxiety. One rural Oklahoman reflected on school consolidation: "It creates ghost towns . . . and when that town dies, the church dies. The little industry that's left is gone. And so, all of a sudden, all you have is another memory of the past."[33]

School closures force rural families to make difficult choices: moving away to a town that still has a local school or tolerating long, daily bus rides for their children. The former option can cascade as more families move away, fewer move in, and employers and businesses lose employees and customers. The latter can have detrimental effects on students' quality of life, learning time, and extracurricular opportunities.

If consolidation is one threat, geographic distance from centers of decision-making authority is another. Especially in the South, districts are often coterminous with counties. While the central office of an urban district may be just a walk or bus ride away, rural stakeholders are often far removed from the county seat where the board of education makes key decisions.

The mere distance makes it difficult for district leaders to stay in touch with the challenges and opportunities in each individual community within its boundaries. And, even if district leaders are in touch, they must still balance the demands of disparate communities and make difficult decisions about schools' viability. It's reasonable to think that some rural stakeholders will be left dissatisfied by district decisions.

As demonstrated in Crestone, Colorado, and Graysville, Indiana, rural charter schools can provide a mechanism for local communities to take greater responsibility and control over their local school—perhaps because the district office has slated their school for closure, because they disagree with the decisions that are being made on behalf of their community, or because they have a vision for a unique school model that matches the needs and values of their particular population.

The path to sustain a rural charter school as a local community school is certainly not an easy one, but it can allow a community to maintain a school as its center and provide local-level governance for its design, sustainability, and governance.

## Charter Conversion: Using the Chartering Mechanism to Increase Autonomy and Reduce the Burden of Compliance and Reporting

Converting a rural district school to a charter school can also provide a mechanism for fostering innovation, reducing regulation, and minimizing the burden of reporting requirements. Numerous small, rural schools in Oregon have converted to charter status—in part to take advantage of this increased autonomy.[34]

One such school is in Elkton, Oregon, a small town about fifty miles southwest of Eugene. Ten years ago, the district superintendent predicted its local school would close within three years. Today, Elkton Charter Academy serves 250 students—nearly twice as many as the district school used to.

The district school converted to a charter school in 2010. It serves students in kindergarten through twelfth grade, of whom 57 percent are economically disadvantaged and receives a four out of five on the state's accountability system for both growth and achievement.[35]

As covered in *The Oregonian*, charter conversion is "a little-used clause in the charter school law, but becoming more common." As a charter school, Elkton has been able to access federal grants for charter schools and operates with fewer state requirements.[36]

Elkton Charter Academy has used its newfound autonomy well. It has established an innovative curriculum based on the natural resources within walking distance of the school building and now attracts students from across five surrounding school districts. While surrounding districts have been critical of the school for enrolling their students, school leader Mike Hughes has said, "Kids can leave as fast as they come. Going this way, we have to stay on top of our game. . . . If you don't do something unique, you won't survive."[37]

Elkton Charter Academy and others like it in Oregon and across the country benefit from increased autonomy from federal and state law. Federal and state law restricts how schools operate—from daily schedules to procurement policies, staffing decisions, use of funds, and curriculum and instruction. These regulations are often designed with more urban settings in mind and can be a poor fit for the unique challenges in rural communities. Too often, they prevent rural schools from establishing programs that meet the unique needs of their students.

One example is the numerous teacher-evaluation policies that states enacted over the past ten years. Designed to embolden school leaders to dismiss ineffective staff, these policies are often poorly applied to rural districts with small talent pools, where dismissing a teacher may not be nearly as hard as finding another person to fill the role.

In addition, rural schools struggle with associated reporting requirements. Because of the small number of students in many rural districts, a school superintendent may also be the principal and bus driver—with few support staff and little time for filling out grant applications or compliance reports. Indeed, in a 2013 survey, rural superintendents ranked "paperwork and compliance requirements" as the number two issue facing rural districts.[38] One superintendent said, "I'm it! I don't have any support staff like the guys running the large districts. They can delegate the work to staff. But I have to turn in the same reports as they do. It takes a lot of time."[39]

Charter schools are hardly free from reporting requirements, and regulatory burdens and compliance reporting vary state to state. But, on average, they are better off than district schools.[40] With fewer and less burdensome requirements, charter schools can spend less time and resources fulfilling them and more time focusing on serving students—and converting to a charter school can provide small rural schools with these same benefits.

Charter schools were originally conceived as way to give schools more autonomy, and status as a charter school can help insulate rural schools like Elkton Charter Academy from policies that do not fit their constraints and circumstances.

## To Meet the Needs of Specific Student Populations: Charter Schools Can Specialize in Ways That District Schools Cannot

The smaller size of student populations in rural areas does not mean that rural schools serve students with less diverse needs. Rural school districts often serve very disadvantaged populations with very specific needs—such as intergenerational and deep poverty, a strong attachment to and desire to preserve tribal culture, or seasonal migration. A rural community may have a large number of young adults who need additional education to achieve a GED and/or enroll in college courses, a population of Native American families who have specific cultural traditions and languages they want to preserve for the next generation, or an influx of migrant students with limited English proficiency who need specific and intensive interventions on an alternative daily or yearly schedule.

It was just such a unique and pressing need that inspired the Farmworker Institute of Educational and Leadership Development (FIELD) to found Escuela Popular Instituto Campesino (EPIC) de Cesar Chavez High School.[41] According to FIELD's analysis, about half of recent immigrants from Mexico in their communities have the equivalent of a sixth-grade level of education. Nearly one in three are illiterate in their native language. FIELD has established a number of educational initiatives—one of which is EPIC de Cesar Chavez High School—to address these stark realities.

EPIC de Cesar Chavez High School is a charter school with locations in fourteen rural towns across California, founded as part of FIELD's mission to empower the underserved. It received its charter from the Nevada County Board of Education in 2014 and serves 310 adult students in twelfth grade only.[42] Most students either previously dropped out of high school and/or are recent immigrants who received whatever education they have in their country of origin. Nearly nine out of ten students are Hispanic or Latino, and 62 percent are English language learners. Classes are offered in the morning and evening hours, and students range in age from eighteen years old to some in their sixties.[43]

Many of the students in the high school previously participated in FIELD's English literacy program, which serves about 8,000 people, and were identified for their potential and desire to earn a high school diploma. But FIELD and EPIC de Cesar Chavez High School aim to do a lot more than provide their students with a diploma. As FIELD president and CEO David Villarino stated, "The goal isn't to just train or educate people; it's to use that training and education to . . . give them the confidence and skills to run their own businesses." Because rural communities don't have the same economic opportunities as urban communities, FIELD and EPIC de Cesar Chavez High School are empowering students to create their own.

That work is about to take off. In mid-November 2017, FIELD and EPIC de Cesar Chavez High School received a $1.3 million grant from the California Department of Education to advance their efforts to facilitate entrepreneurship among their graduates. In partnership with numerous higher-education institutions in California, FIELD and EPIC de Cesar Chavez High School will build career pathways and foster entrepreneurship in conservation, agriculture, and early childhood education.[44]

In its work to date, EPIC de Cesar Chavez High School has confronted some of the operational challenges common among rural charter schools; FIELD president and CEO David Villarino indicates that attracting and retaining teachers is the "biggest single challenge they have." Notably, however, the school has not faced resistance from the local district. "This is an expansion of resources for students of that age group, who did not have the opportunity to graduate from high school," Superintendent Louise Johnson said at the time of the school's charter approval.[45]

Rather than competing with the existing school system for resources, EPIC de Cesar Chavez High School was able to tap additional resources from the state to serve a specific student population with a specialized educational program.

EPIC de Cesar Chavez High School is just one example of how a rural charter school may be able to serve unique student populations in ways that district schools cannot. Districts may not have a program for adult students, or the capacity to build one. The Native American population in the district may be too small to sway key decision makers to support a culturally supportive environment for their children. A different yearly or daily schedule for migrant children may place too much strain on existing routines and infrastructure. In these circumstances, a specially designed charter school may be just what's needed.


## POLICY RECOMMENDATIONS

Rural charter schools are hardly a straightforward policy salve. The political and operational challenges that stymie the growth of rural charters are real and not for the faint of heart. And yet, there are numerous instances in which rural charter schools have added real value to their communities—offering families alternatives to struggling district schools, preserving a community's school in the face of consolidation, providing increased autonomy from burdensome regulations, or serving special populations.

Navigating the tension between the constraints and opportunities of rural charter schools requires knowledge of the challenges, belief in the opportunity, and attention to local capacity and circumstance.

The first step in the process is to clear the brush so that rural charter schools are, at least, an available option. That is, state policymakers must remove policy barriers to rural charter schools. First, state policymakers should remove blunt prohibitions of rural charter schools, including any statutory limits on the percentage of district students who enroll in charter schools (often capped at 5, 10, or 15 percent).

States with laws that limit charters to specific urban centers, or to districts with a minimum number of schools, students, or residents should also strike those provisions from their books. This doesn't mean that charter schools *will* open in rural communities; it simply creates the option and puts the decision in the hands of local communities and authorizers.

Second, with decision-making authority in the hands of local communities and authorizers, policymakers, analysts, and authorizer-support organizations must help build their capacity to assess the potential for a rural charter school. Authorizers, in particular, need resources and guidance on how to adjust their assessment of a charter school's financial viability, educational program, and community engagement—including whether and how these standards should differ when evaluating an application for a rural versus an urban school.

Once we allow local communities and charter-school authorizers the opportunity to assess rural charter schools on a case-by-case basis, we must also provide them with the technical knowledge and skills to determine whether a rural charter school is a reasonable option for providing greater educational opportunity to those who need it.

Third, policymakers should continue to push against barriers to charter-school growth that apply across geographies, but which particularly affect the viability of rural charters: inequitable per-pupil funding and access to facilities or facilities financing. Students who attend charter schools deserve the same public support as those who attend district schools—and equalizing charter funding and facilities access is especially important to improving the ability of innovative leaders to make their models work with limited economies of scale.

Once state policymakers and practitioners have removed these barriers to rural charter schools, they should also support and incentivize the growth of charter schools where they can meet the needs of rural communities.

First, state policymakers should ensure that charter schools are permitted to serve and enroll specific student populations. Many state charter-school laws restrict whether charter schools can have enrollment criteria to target specific student populations. For instance, EPIC de Cesar Chavez High School is able to focus on adult students because California's charter law allows schools to define enrollment preferences with their authorizers.

While more states are beginning to define a broader set of permissible enrollment preferences (or allowing authorizers to define them), many states lack this flexibility. Policymakers should ensure that targeted enrollment preferences are available so that they can be leveraged and assessed effectively at the authorizer and school level.

Second, state policymakers should ensure that charter schools can enroll students across district boundaries. Many states require charter schools to enroll students only from within their districts of residence. But, in rural areas of the country, the ability of a rural charter school to draw students from across multiple districts can dilute their impact on district schools and allow for a more sustainable and diversified source of student enrollment.

Finally, and again aligned with the charter movement writ large, policymakers must protect the autonomy–accountability bargain at the heart of the charter-school concept. For rural charter schools in particular, maximum autonomy from burdensome regulations and compliance reporting (in exchange for accountability for student outcomes) will enable rural-district schools to convert to charters, reduce overhead expenses, sustain financial viability, and build innovative programs responsive to local needs.

It bears reiterating that rural charter schools have risks. They are not a panacea and should not be undertaken without serious consideration of the operational challenges and constraints. But nor should they be dismissed as a purely urban phenomenon. Instead, policymakers, practitioners, and stakeholders must wrestle with the murky middle ground and allow that sometimes a rural charter school may be just what's needed.

## CONCLUSION

When thinking of the challenges of rural education, charter schools are rarely the first strategy that comes to mind. The challenges to establishing a rural charter school can be politically and operationally prohibitive. First, the founders of a rural charter school must start from scratch in explaining to their communities what a charter school is (and isn't). They are also likely to have an uphill climb politically, with few charter advocates focused on rural issues and ready-made opposition. Finally, when the political stars do align, the lack of start-up funding, lean budgets, and limited access to human capital present significant operational hurdles to overcome.

The challenges are daunting, and the stakes are high. A successful rural charter school cannot only provide students with improved educational opportunity but also help revitalize and sustain a struggling community. Failure can leave a community without any school at all. Given the challenges and the risks, it is important to pursue the expansion of rural charter schools cautiously.

Unfortunately, too many state policies prevent community and school leaders from even considering them. State policymakers should remove barriers to rural charter schools, support the expertise and capacity of local communities and authorizers to assess viability, and ensure that charters have access to equitable funds and facilities.

Policymakers can also make state laws more amenable to the unique ways in which charter schools can provide opportunity in rural areas, by increasing flexibility in serving special student populations, granting charter schools the ability to enroll students across district boundaries, and protecting the autonomy-accountability bargain at the heart of charter schooling.

Finally, there is more work to be done across the education community to support rural charter schools. To more fully explore their potential, additional analysis is needed to identify trends in successful (and unsuccessful) rural charter schools. What are the conditions in which rural charter schools have been successful or unsuccessful? What barriers should rural charter school founders be prepared to address?

More study is also needed to help authorizers, community leaders, and stakeholders assess the potential and viability for a charter school in a rural community. How should authorizers determine the level of community support for a charter school, and how much should it weigh in their decisions? What extra financial precautions should authorizers look for, and how do the financial models for a rural school differ from those for urban charters?

More analysis is needed on what other school-improvement strategies rural charter schools can enable. In the numerous other challenges and opportunities in rural education—such as teacher recruitment and retention, career and technical education, postsecondary access, and personalized learning—how might rural charter schools be positioned to pilot new efforts or support student success? Like their urban counterparts, rural charter schools may be positioned to pilot new innovations, challenge convention, or produce student outcomes that reshape the sector's perspectives on what's possible.

## NOTES

1  Note: Author's calculations are based on 2014–2015 Common Core of Data. See https://nces.ed.gov/ccd/.

2  Center for Research on Education Outcomes, "The Urban Charter School Study," 2015, http://urbancharters.stanford.edu/overview.php.

3   Brian Gill, "The Effect of Charter Schools on Students in Traditional Public
    Schools: A Review of the Evidence," Education Next, November 2, 2016,
    http://educationnext.org/the-effect-of-charter-schools-on-students-in-traditional-
    public-schools-a-review-of-the-evidence/.

4   Note: Author's calculations are based on 2014–2015 Common Core of Data. See
    https://nces.ed.gov/ccd/.

5   Ibid.

6   U.S. Department of Education, Office of Innovation and Improvement, "Charter
    Schools Program Overview," December 2015, https://www2.ed.gov/programs/
    charter/cspdata.pdf; and U.S. Department of Education, Office of Innovation and
    Improvement, "Notice Inviting Applications for New Awards Fiscal Year (FY)
    2010," *Federal Register* 75, no. 2010–6370 (March 23, 2010), 13735, https://www.
    federalregister.gov/documents/2010/03/23/2010-6370/office-of-innovation-
    and-improvement-overview-information-charter-schools-program-csp-state.

7   "Investing in Cities," Walton Family Foundation, accessed November 28, 2017,
    http://www.waltonfamilyfoundation.org/our-impact/k12-education/investing-in-
    cities; "The Broad Prize for Public Charter Schools," The Eli and Edythe Broad
    Foundation, November 28, 2017, http://broadfoundation.org/the-broad-prize-
    for-public-charter-schools/; "Charter and Parochial Schools," The Louis Calder
    Foundation, accessed November 28, 2017, https://www.louiscalderfoundation.
    org/grant-program/charter-parochial-schools; and "National Fund," Charter
    School Growth Fund, accessed November 28, 2017, https://chartergrowthfund.
    org/portfolio/national-fund/.

8   Marguerite Roza, "Innovation Amid Financial Scarcity: The Opportunity
    in Rural Schools, Rural Opportunities Consortium of Idaho," February
    2015, 5, http://www.rociidaho.org/wp-content/uploads/2015/02/ROCI_2015_
    InnovationAmidScarcity_Final.pdf.

9   Meagan Batdorff, Larry Maloney, Jay F. May, Sheree T. Speakman, Patrick
    J. Wolf, Albert Cheng, "Foreword," in Charter School Funding: Inequity Expands,
    University of Arkansas Department of Education Reform, April 2014, http://
    www.uaedreform.org/wp-content/uploads/charter-funding-inequity-expands.pdf.

10  Daniel Player, "The Supply and Demand for Rural Teachers, Rural Opportunities
    Consortium of Idaho," March 2015, 5–11, http://www.rociidaho.org/wp-content/
    uploads/2015/03/ROCI_2015_RuralTeachers_FINAL.pdf.

11  Juliet Squire and Kelly Robson, "Voices from Rural Oklahoma: Where's Edu-
    cation Headed on the Plain?," Bellwether Education Partners, February 18,
    2017, 30, https://bellwethereducation.org/publication/voices-rural-oklahoma-
    wheres-education-headed-plain.

12  Education Next and the Harvard Program on Education Policy and Governance,
    "The 2017 EdNext Poll on School Reform: Public Thinking on School Choice,
    Common Core, Higher Ed, and More," 2017, 10, http://educationnext.org/
    files/2017ednextpoll.pdf.

13  Note: Maine and New Hampshire restrict charter schools to no more than
    5 percent–10 percent of a school's existing students per grade level, effectively
    limiting charter growth in rural areas; New Mexico has a similar constraint for

districts with 1,300 or fewer students; Missouri limits charter schools to Kansas City and St. Louis; Oklahoma has a cap of five charter schools per year in counties with fewer than 500,000 residents; Utah law requires that priority be given to charter schools opening in areas with growing populations; see Todd Ziebarth, Louann Bierlein Palmer, and Emily Schultz, "Measuring Up to the Model: A Ranking of State Charter Public School Laws," National Alliance for Public Charter Schools, March 2017, http://www.publiccharters.org/wp-content/uploads/2017/03/MODEL-Report_FINAL.pdf?x87663.

14  Note: Author's calculations based on 2014–2015 Common Core of Data. See https://nces.ed.gov/ccd/.

15  Note: I reviewed all nineteen state-level analyses from CREDO since 2009. Of these, nine studies reported charter school impact by geography. From eighteen data points (math and reading in each of nine states), rural charter schools show a positive impact in seven, a negative impact in eight, and no statistically significant impact in three. See Center for Research on Education Outcomes, "Charter School Studies," various dates, http://credo.stanford.edu/research-reports.html.

16  National Alliance for Public Charter Schools, "A Call to Action to Improve the Quality of Full-time Virtual Charter Public Schools," June 2016, 2, http://www.publiccharters.org/wp-content/uploads/2016/06/Virtuals-FINAL-06202016-1.pdf?x87663.

17  Federal Communications Commission, "2016 Broadband Progress Report," January 29, 2016, https://www.fcc.gov/reports-research/reports/broadband-progress-reports/2016-broadband-progress-report.

18  Center for Research on Education Outcomes, "Online Charter School Study," 2015, 23, https://credo.stanford.edu/pdfs/Online%20Charter%20Study%20Final.pdf.

19  Jennifer Schiess and Andrew Rotherham, "Big Country: How Variations in High School Graduation Plans Impact Rural Students, Rural Opportunities Consortium of Idaho," October 2015, 28, http://www.rociidaho.org/wp-content/uploads/2015/10/ROCI_HSRigor_Final.pdf.

20  Daniel Player, "Take Me Home Country Road? Exploring the College Attendance Patters of Rural Youth, Rural Opportunities Consortium of Idaho," July 2015, Figure 5, http://www.rociidaho.org/wp-content/uploads/2015/07/ROCI_Rural-College-Patterns_Final.pdf.

21  Ibid., Figure 11.

22  National Student Clearinghouse Research Center, "National College Progression Rates," October 15, 2017, https://nscrescarchcenter.org/wp-content/uploads/HighSchoolBenchmarks2013.pdf.

23  Note: Unless otherwise noted, information regarding the Academy of Seminole is from author's interview with Paul Campbell, October 2016, and e-mail correspondence with author, November 14, 2017.

24  Oklahoma Department of Education, "2017 Low Income Report w/ Percentages," 2017, 68, http://sde.ok.gov/sde/child-nutrition-documents#Low-Income.

25  Oklahoma Department of Education, "2016 Report Card: Seminole," 2016, http://afreportcards.ok.gov/.

26  Ben Felder, "Seminole Charter School Delayed One Year," *Oklahoman*, May 26, 2017, http://newsok.com/article/5550604.

27  Max Marchitello, "Betsy DeVos Has a Rural Problem," *USA Today*, February 2, 2017, https://www.usatoday.com/story/opinion/2017/02/02/devos-rural-america-school-reform-column/97362016/.

28  Terry Ryan and Paul T. Hill, "In a Changing America, What Can Charter Schools Offer?," Brown Center Chalkboard, May 22, 2017, https://www.brookings.edu/blog/brown-center-chalkboard/2017/05/22/in-a-changing-rural-america-what-can-charter-schools-offer/.

29  Crestone Charter School, "CCS History—How the Crestone Charter School Started," accessed November 28, 2017, https://crestone-charter-school.org/index.php/about-us/ccs-history; and Colorado Department of Education, "School Dashboard Crestone Charter School—Moffat 2," Growth Tab, accessed December 7, 2017, http://www2.cde.state.co.us/schoolview/dish/schooldashboard.asp.

30  Katie Ash, "Rural Charter Schools Face Special Challenges," *Education Week*, May 6, 2014, https://www.edweek.org/ew/articles/2014/05/07/30rural_ep.h33.html.

31  Indiana Department of Education, "School and Corporation Reports: Rural Community Academy (7951)," 2017, https://compass.doe.in.gov/dashboard/overview.aspx?type=school&id=7951; and National Alliance for Public Charter Schools, "The Story of Rural Charter Schools," January 27, 2014, https://www.youtube.com/watch?v=4bZMzvWyau4&t=185s.

32  National Conference of State Legislatures, "School and District Consolidation," March 14, 2011, http://www.ncsl.org/research/education/school-and-district-consolidation.aspx.

33  Squire and Robson, "Voices from Rural Oklahoma," 28.

34  Kimberly Melton, "Oregon's Rural Schools Look to Charter Status to Survive," December 17, 2010, *Oregonian*, http://www.oregonlive.com/education/index.ssf/2010/12/oregons_rural_schools_look_to.html.

35  Oregon Department of Education, "School and District Report Cards: School Year 2016–2017," accessed November 28, 2017, http://www.oregon.gov/ode/schools-and-districts/reportcards/reportcards/Pages/Accountability-Measures.aspx; and Oregon Department of Education, "Oregon Report Card: Elkton SD 34," 2017, http://www.ode.state.or.us/data/reportcard/reports.aspx.

36  Melton, "Oregon's Rural Schools."

37  Ibid.

38  Lars D. Johnson, Ashley LiBetti Mitchel, and Andrew J. Rotherham, "Federal Education Policy in Rural America, Rural Opportunities Consortium of Idaho," December 2014, 20, http://www.rociidaho.org/wp-content/uploads/2015/01/ROCI_2014FedEdPolicy_FINAL_0115.pdf.

39  Paul T. Hill, "States Could Do More for Rural Education," 7, in *The SEA of the Future: Uncovering the Productivity Promise of Rural Education*, eds. Bethany Gross and Ashley Jochim (Austin, TX: Building State Capacity and Productivity Center, May 2015), http://www.elabs10.com/content/2010000862/SEAF4-FINAL.pdf.

40 Dana Brinson and Jacob Rosch, "Charter School Autonomy: A Half-Broken Promise?," Thomas B. Fordham Institute, April 2010, http://edex.s3-us-west-2. amazonaws.com/publication/pdfs/Charter%20School%20Autonomy%20-%20 May%202010_8.pdf.

41 Note: Unless otherwise noted, information is from author's interview with David Villarino, CEO and president of FIELD, November 9, 2017. For more information about FIELD, see https://www.farmworkerinstitute.org/.

42 California Department of Education, "Enrollment Report: 2016–17 Enrollment by Grade," 2017, http://dq.cde.ca.gov/dataquest/dqcensus/enrgrdlevels. aspx?agglevel=School&year=2016-17&cds=29102980130823.

43 Cory Fisher, "A Diploma at Any Age: Adult High School Founded by Cesar Chavez Targets Rural Immigrant Workers," *Union*, December 19, 2016, http:// www.theunion.com/news/local-news/a-diploma-at-any-age/.

44 Sarah Thompson, "The Cesar E. Chavez Founded FIELD Institute Receives $1.3 Million from State Board of Education to Develop Programs," *Daily Telescope*, November 13, 2017, http://dailytelescope.com/pr/the-cesar-e-chavez-founded-field-institute-receives-1-3-million-from-state-board-of-education-to-develop-programs/9988.

45 KNCO News Talk 830, "County Board of Education Approves New Charter School," April 10, 2014, https://knco.com/county-board-of-education-approves-new-charter-school/.

# Conclusion

## Michael Q. McShane and
## Andy Smarick

When it comes to poverty, politics, and social pressures, there can be significant overlap in the issues faced by educators across the varied geographies of the United States. In fact, a major lesson that can be culled from the various chapters of this volume is that one fruitful way to engage with the subject of rural education is to start with shared strengths and struggles and then, when considering ways to amplify rural schools' benefits and address their shortcomings, consider differences.

In other words, discussions about rural schools should begin with "schools"—what's common across the K–12 field, regardless of location—and then progress to "rural"—how this geography's characteristics might shape particular programs or priorities.

Because so many education-reform initiatives have focused on cities; because so many education philanthropists, advocates, and researchers are based in cities; and because so many high-needs students live in cities, urban America is typically seen as the baseline in conversations about education reform. As a consequence, much like the various official definitions of "rural," the chapters of this volume have often sought first to distinguish these communities from their urban counterparts. This makes a great deal of sense.

And, in truth, this lens can, indeed, prove valuable. With regard to history, culture, teacher recruitment, school choice, and much more, the rural-education experience can be quite different. It is all but impossible to truly understand the practices and policies of rural schools without appreciating these differences.

But before we get to those differences and their implications for rural school-specific policy questions, it is worth taking some time to appreciate the commonalities that rural schools share with urban schools, and the lessons that can be learned from their similar experiences. Once those have been demonstrated and discussed, we can focus on the specific situation of rural schools and what can be done to help them better meet the needs of the children of their communities.

## COMMONALITIES

There are several findings in the chapters of this volume that speak to how rural schooling is quite similar—and, in some cases, surprisingly similar—to schooling in cities, suburbs, and exurbs.

Today, rural areas have poverty rates not terribly different from nonrural areas, and which areas are poorer seems to depend on the definition of "rural" being used. According to the metropolitan definition, rural areas are a bit poorer (including among all age groups). The Census Bureau's definition, however, finds urban areas to be poorer (including among children); the Bureau's supplemental-poverty measure also finds urban areas to be slightly poorer. Both cities and rural communities have millions of students whose families struggle financially, and this fact influences both locales' schools.

Similarly, as Nat Malkus points out in chapter 1, by a number of measures, student achievement in rural areas is like that of other locales. For example, rural pre-K students have reading and math skills that are similar to suburban students. Interestingly, even though rural areas have far less population density, their young children have childcare arrangements similar to those in cities. Special-education rates don't differ much across locales. And rural students perform comparably, with a few differences, on the National Assessment of Educational Progress (NAEP).

An important political similarity between rural and urban areas is the shadow cast by the Progressive-Era reformers of a century ago. As Sara Dahill-Brown and Ashley Jochim argue in chapter 4, many Progressives distrusted the decision-making of local leaders—in cities and rural communities, alike—and wanted to professionalize and systematize schools. This both frustrated local residents by eroding their decision-making power and bred distrust of outsiders who believed that they knew better than local leaders.

In an interesting corollary, both rural areas and cities appear to exhibit higher levels of *internal* agreement. Members of rural and city school boards were not likely to report high levels of conflict or personal disagreement among members. The conflict arises when outsiders, from the state capital or Washington, DC, show up and start telling them what to do. It seems that there is a particularly pronounced sense across city and rural leaders that "we" know our communities' schools and "they" don't.

In terms of operations and governance, there are also a number of key commonalities. The vast majority of public school students in cities and in rural communities still attend schools run by their local school districts. Both rural and city schools are deeply engaged in school-funding debates (e.g., how much money is enough, how much should local governments contribute vis-à-vis the state government).

In fact, a combination of state policies often leads to rural and urban public schools receiving subsidies from the state's suburban and exurban areas. And rural schools are quite similar, find Daniel Player and Aliza Husain in chapter 7, to urban schools when it comes to the number and types of teacher vacancies reported.

All in all, then, across these different geographies, traditional districts still dominate public education; they struggle similarly with poverty and report comparable achievement results; and their leaders face common financial and staffing issues and have historically been skeptical of the authority of outsiders.

## DIFFERENCES

With this understanding, we can better appreciate rural schools' differences and why they matter.

### Diversity

One of the most important features of rural schools is the very different types of communities they serve. Obviously, cities are scattered across the nation, each possessing a particular history. But, big cities also share important characteristics: population density, variety of employers, cultural amenities, and so on. But, "rural" encompasses areas as different as farming towns in the Midwest to villages in New England to Native-American reservations in the Southwest to African-American communities in the Deep South.

In some cases, an issue is consistent across these various locales (e.g., sparse population); but, in other cases, the differences are material. For instance, the Deep South is still influenced by the legacy of slavery and segregation in a way that New England is not, as Sheneka M. Williams demonstrates in chapter 2. Throughout this volume, we saw these intra-rural similarities and difference manifest in a number of ways (related to poverty, employment, family structure, and more). One important example was demographics.

In general, rural schools have fewer minority students. These national averages, however, disguise regional differences: In the Northeast and Midwest, rural schools are whiter than nonrural schools, but in the South, rural schools have more black students than nonrural schools. In the West, they have more Hispanic students than nonrural schools. These regional differences are also seen in poverty numbers. City students in the Northeast and Midwest are poorer than their rural peers, and those city students score lower on NAEP.

## Community

One of the most striking findings is that rural schools have higher high school graduation rates than all other locales. However, rural students have lower college-going rates. A complex set of factors are at play here, including the proximity and cost of higher-education institutions, the types of nearby jobs available, and, interestingly, the expectations of families: Adults in rural areas are less educated than urban adults, and a lower percentage of rural parents expect their kids to earn college degrees. Rural-district superintendents are also less likely than their urban peers to believe that college attendance is an important indicator of school success.

And these facts can have troubling ripple effects.

If today's rural students remain less likely to graduate from college and have a greater chance of ending up as low-income adults, they could ultimately have significant employment problems: Poor people in nonmetropolitan areas work less than their metropolitan counterparts. Moreover, the goods-producing industries that often support rural communities (e.g., farming, forestry, manufacturing) are increasingly being replaced by lower-paying service jobs.

In total, today's rural students may end up, when compared to their suburban and urban peers, as less educated, less likely to work, and more likely to have lower-wage jobs. This could ultimately exacerbate the problem of intergenerational poverty in rural America: Today, 85 percent of "persistently poor" counties are rural.

But rural students also have a number of advantages. Rural adults are more likely to be married, and rural children are more likely to live with two parents than students in cities. Rural families are more likely to be engaged in school and community activities. They are also likelier to attend church and sporting events than many of their peers.

Another key difference for rural areas is the "brain drain"—that, since opportunities in sparsely populated areas are limited and employment risk can be high (e.g., 70 percent of rural counties are dependent on a particular industry), many high-achieving students leave after high school graduation and don't return. Indeed, some research finds that outward migration from rural counties supports intergenerational upward mobility. And, as noted in chapter 4, two-thirds of rural communities lost population between 2010 and 2014.

At the same time, rural students are less likely to go to museums, libraries, and concerts. This is key because rural students also have less access to other opportunities. Their schools have fewer specialized services, like academic-enrichment activities, Advanced Placement courses, and foreign-language offerings.

Rural areas also have fewer specialty schools, like those focused on career and technical education. Indeed, chapter 2 gave voice to the isolation-from-opportunity felt by rural students. Rural kids, on average, may enter school with a number of family and social-capital advantages, but these can be offset by fewer opportunities inside of their schools' walls.

Part of the explanation for the limited number of extras is that rural schools are generally smaller than schools in other areas. With fewer students on average, these schools seem to be unable to benefit from some of the economies of scale that come with larger districts and schools. The flip side of this coin, though, is that rural schools have more adults—both teachers and administrators—per student than schools elsewhere.

Among the saddest differences between rural and city schools—chronicled by Clayton Hale and Sally Satel in chapter 3—is the devastating influence the opioid crisis has had on the former. To be sure, other addiction epidemics, like crack cocaine, have devastated urban communities, and cities have not been immune to opioid addiction. But the effects in rural communities can be staggering.

For example, largely rural states including West Virginia, New Hampshire, Ohio, and Kentucky have among the nation's highest rates of fatal opioid overdoses. Suffering from the physical pain stemming from careers in manual labor and the psychic pain associated with massive job losses, isolation, and cultural change, rural America seems to have been especially vulnerable to the lures of OxyContin, fentanyl, and similar drugs.

Although rural students don't seem to be using at disproportionately high rates, the use by the adults in their lives is affecting them, often dramatically. When parents and guardians overdose or are arrested, kids suffer badly, and their schools must help pick up the pieces. Teachers and administrators are spending resources to find temporary guardians, get children to and from school, help the students cope with the trauma, and much more. In some states, the number of children living in state care is skyrocketing. And we must worry about the long-term effects of adults' addiction on the affected children.

## Funding

State-level funding policies also affect rural schools in unusual ways. As explained by James V. Shuls in chapter 6, state governments often assess agricultural land at lower values in order to protect farm communities. So, even if all of a state's school districts set an identical local property-tax rate, rural communities would still generate less local revenue for schools (based on the actual market value of property). In 2017, Missouri collected more than $7.2 billion in property taxes, but less than 2 percent came from agricultural property taxes even though two-thirds of the state's 44.7 million acres are considered farmland.

This isn't unique to Missouri. As Shuls notes, one study found that for some Ohio communities, properties are assessed at a rate about 80 percent lower than the land's market value. The impact of such policies is stark: In Missouri, suburban and city districts contribute more than 60 percent of per-pupil expenditures, but rural and town districts contribute only about 45 percent. As a result, state governments provide more per-pupil dollars to rural areas—meaning dollars from nonrural communities are used by the state government to subsidize rural schools.

But, importantly, these results are also attributable to some local rural decisions. Rural towns could tax themselves at higher rates to compensate for the lower property assessments. But they don't always do so. In fact, in Missouri, of the sixty-four school districts taxing themselves at the state-minimum level, sixty-two are either rural or town school districts. These districts wouldn't lose state subsidies by taxing themselves at a higher rate since the state's contribution level is based on the district's *ability* to contribute, not its decision on how much to contribute.

## Politics

The lack of access to community amenities and in-school resources speaks to a larger issue: that rural communities can see themselves as outsiders and lacking power. As a number of our chapters noted, studies of rural schools—especially studies of African-American students in the South—are conspicuously underrepresented in the academic literature. More rural residents see themselves as blue-collar and working or lower class. Only about a quarter of rural residents think urban communities share their values.

And rural communities differ politically, as well. For example, 75 percent of districts serving rural areas were in counties that supported Romney over Obama, while just 41 percent of districts serving cities were in counties where Romney earned more votes that Obama. And 91 percent of remote-rural districts were in counties that supported Trump over Clinton.

These issues help explain why charter schools are far less prevalent in rural areas; although there are about 4,000 urban charters, there are fewer than 800 rural charters. Since many rural areas are sparsely populated and/or losing population, charter laws' primary purpose—enabling the creation of new schools—can be seen as less of an attribute than a liability.

In a big city of a million people and hundreds of schools, the addition of one new school can be little noticed. But in a small town with one school that educates all kids and serves a wide array of community functions, an additional school can be destabilizing.

## Staffing

One key difference that influences the day-to-day work of rural schools is that they can face particular challenges when it comes to recruiting staff. Rural areas can be isolated, lack attractive housing options, cultural amenities, and job opportunities for teachers' spouses. Moreover, since teachers often choose to work in areas close to where they attended high school and rural areas have lower college-graduation rates, rural communities can have smaller pools of candidates. So, although rural schools report less difficulty filling general elementary-education positions (the most common role) than urban schools, they have more difficulty filling STEM and ELL positions.

This challenge is particularly pronounced in remote rural areas. One interesting possibility raised in chapter 7 is that if rural areas were as selective as other geographies in choosing teachers, they might report even more difficulty (e.g., rural teachers are less likely to have graduated from a selective college and less likely to possess a master's degree).

## MOVING FORWARD

Perhaps the key high-level takeaway from these chapters is that rural and urban (and suburban) schools face many of the same issues, but because of the particular characteristics of rural areas, they often have to handle these issues in different ways. For policymakers, an important lesson is that laws, regulations, and programs need to provide rural leaders with the flexibility necessary to address their specific, and occasionally unusual, contexts.

For example, because of a particular tangle of out-of-school issues—loss of population, reliance on a single industry, low levels of college completion among adults—a rural school's efforts to raise achievement levels might look different than those in other geographies. Angela Rachidi argued in chapter 5 that, to improve schools, rural communities need to consider economic development and efforts to strengthen local labor markets. But, for another locale, investments in new schools and principal training might be the better bet.

Families in rural communities could very well prize the concept of school choice as dearly as families in cities. But because of extenuating circumstances, today's charter laws haven't led rural America to embrace chartering as urban areas have.

Juliet Squire made the case in chapter 8 that different approaches to chartering might better fit rural communities. For example, instead of creating a vast supply of new schools, charter laws could help rural areas convert existing district schools into charters so that educators have more autonomy; allow a rural community to replace a school being closed by a district; and enable families to create programs tightly tailored to the needs of specific student populations.

Chapter 1 made clear that even if America embarked on a massive effort to help rural schools, the vast variation within the category of "rural schools" would require state and local leaders to differentiate their strategies greatly. In some areas, rural schools are almost entirely white; in others, they are overwhelmingly African American or Hispanic. In some regions, rural students outperform nonrural students; in others, it's the opposite. In some states, rural areas have depressed economies and intergenerational poverty; in others, job prospects and economic mobility are more positive.

Rural schools, like schools elsewhere, have deep concerns about funding. But because state legislatures have made the protection of agricultural land a policy priority, they've written property-assessment rules that make raising local funds more difficult. Moreover, for a host of reasons, some rural areas are less willing to tax themselves to support schools. As a result, state and local policymakers need to find creative ways to balance different rural priorities, rural voting preferences, and the need to adequately support rural schools.

All schools worry about filling job vacancies—it's an annual challenge, and, for some districts, it means hiring hundreds or thousands of educators during a relatively quick timeframe. But rural areas, because they often have fewer cultural amenities and fewer local job opportunities for the nonteaching spouses of candidates, can have a tougher time recruiting.

And all schools need to address students' out-of-school challenges; but the specific conditions of rural life today seem to have made these communities especially susceptible to the opioid-addiction crisis and the "deaths of despair" mentioned by several of our authors.

As a last example, rural and urban areas alike can resent the presumptuous meddling of outsiders in their schools, a phenomenon that can be traced back at least to the Progressive Era. But the nature of rural areas' frustration can be quite different. Rural citizens have a heightened sense that outsiders don't know enough about rural communities and that they don't share rural values. Because rural areas are more conservative and have different policy preferences, they can be especially hostile to federal interventions.

So well-meaning, "expert" teams of city-based philanthropists or policy leaders with advice on how to "modernize" rural schools might face deep-seated, long-standing antagonism that seems inconceivable to those hoping to help. While locally developed and locally led efforts in school reform are generally the best received, they may be especially important in rural contexts.

But wrestling with these questions also requires a deeper reflection on the purpose of rural education in these first decades of the twenty-first century. With respect to workforce development, are schools tasked with training students to succeed in the industries that still exist in rural areas or could be moving to rural areas in the near future? Or are schools supposed to prepare students to leave rural areas to head to cities with better job prospects?

This is particularly difficult, because it is impossible to predict the future and know what industries will populate rural communities in the next ten, twenty, or thirty years. But it also strikes at the core of deep, unsettled questions about the goals of our education system and its relationship to the cultural and political communities in which schools operate. The "brain drain" is both a virtuous and vicious cycle, powerfully positive for the individuals who take advantage of it and devastating to those it leaves behind.

Over the past twenty years, K–12 school reform had a decidedly national flare. Big national challenges—low standards, drop-out factories, lagging test scores, falling behind international peers—were identified and roundly criticized. Big national initiatives—No Child Left Behind, Common Core, teacher-evaluation reform, school turnarounds—were launched. They were led by our largest, most powerful national actors, like major foundations and the federal government.

Although much of America's schooling community ultimately bristled at this approach, it might've been doubly frustrating for rural America. Much of the analysis and advocacy was conducted by and much of the programming was led by those who knew too little about rural communities. Not surprisingly, much of the language used to describe the challenges and many of the initiatives designed to be solutions didn't reflect the experience of rural leaders and families.

If America is to take again a national approach to school reform, we should certainly be more mindful of engaging rural America in the problem-definition and reform-development process. But, with the passage of the federal Every Student Succeeds Act and the general view that Uncle Sam had gotten too big for his britches, more power is being returned to state capitals.

Perhaps from that closer-to-home perch it will be easier to make use of this volume's thrust: Understanding rural schools means better appreciating the challenges they share with their counterparts elsewhere and recognizing that to build on rural schools' strengths and help address their challenges, we must respect how and why they are different.

# Index

# About the Editors

**Michael Q. McShane** is director of national research at EdChoice. His analyses and commentary have been published widely in the media, including in the *Huffington Post*, *National Affairs*, *USA Today*, and the *Washington Post*. He has also been featured in education-specific outlets such as *Teachers College Commentary*, *Education Week*, *Phi Delta Kappan*, and *Education Next*. In addition to authoring numerous white papers, Dr. McShane has had academic work published in *Education Finance and Policy* and the *Journal of School Choice*. He is the editor of *New and Better Schools*, author of *Education and Opportunity*, and coeditor of *Teacher Quality 2.0* and *Common Core Meets Education Reform*. A former high school teacher, Dr. McShane is also an adjunct fellow in education policy studies at the American Enterprise Institute (AEI) and a research fellow in the Economic and Policy Analysis Research Center at the University of Missouri.

**Andy Smarick** is the director of civil society, education, and work at the R Street Institute. At the state level, he served as president of the Maryland State Board of Education and deputy commissioner of the New Jersey Department of Education. At the federal lever, he served as an aide at the White House Domestic Policy Council; deputy assistant secretary of planning, evaluation, and policy development at the U.S. Department of Education; and as a legislative assistant to a member of the U.S. House of Representatives. He was also the Morgridge Fellow in Education at the American Enterprise Institute, distinguished visiting fellow at the Thomas B. Fordham Foundation; and partner at Bellwether Education Partners. Among other publications, Mr. Smarick is the author of *The Urban School System of the Future* (Rowman & Littlefield, 2012). He graduated *summa cum laude* and with honors from the University of Maryland, College Park and received a master of public management degree from the University of Maryland's School of Public Policy.

# About the Contributors

**Sara Dahill-Brown** is an assistant professor in the politics and international affairs department at Wake Forest University. She earned her BA from Trinity University and her PhD from the University of Wisconsin–Madison. She has worked as a Texas middle school teacher and as a researcher and volunteer in the school systems of Wisconsin and North Carolina. Her work has appeared in the *Russell Sage Journal of the Social Sciences, Studies in Educational Evaluation,* and *Politics and Policy.* Her current project, which focuses on state approaches to educational governance, is under contract with Harvard Education Press.

**Clayton Hale** is a research associate at the American Enterprise Institute (AEI), where he works closely with Sally Satel on issues surrounding the opioid crisis. He grew up in East Tennessee in a family of educators and has experience with rural health issues, having worked closely with the Tennessee Department of Health. He holds a BA from Johns Hopkins University, where he majored in public health.

**Aliza Husain** is an IES predoctoral fellow in the Education Policy program at the Curry School of Education. She earned her MPP from the Frank Batten School of Leadership and Public Policy in May 2016. After completing her primary education in Karachi, Pakistan, Aliza earned an undergraduate degree in economics from Occidental College. Her current research interests include K–12 teacher quality, teacher retention, and school leadership.

**Ashley Jochim** is a senior research analyst at the Center on Reinventing Public Education (CRPE). Her research focuses on policy analysis and implementation, including work on school turnaround, state education agencies,

K–12 accountability, Common Core standards, and district reform efforts. Before working at CRPE, Dr. Jochim was a graduate fellow at the Center for American Politics and Public Policy and a research analyst at the U.S. Department of Health and Human Services, Office for Civil Rights. She holds a bachelor's degree in political science and psychology and a PhD in political science, both from the University of Washington.

**Nat Malkus** is a research fellow and the deputy director of education policy at AEI, where he specializes in K–12 education. Specifically, he applies quantitative data to education policy. His work focuses on school finance, charter schools, school choice, and the future of standardized testing. Before joining AEI, Dr. Malkus was a senior researcher at the American Institutes for Research, where he led research teams analyzing national education data on topics ranging from how many college students take remedial courses to the comparisons between charter and traditional public schools to tracking student achievement and graduation rates in schools undergoing turnaround reforms. Dr. Malkus has a PhD in education policy and leadership from the University of Maryland, College Park, and a BA in historical studies from Covenant College.

**Daniel Player** is an assistant professor of public policy at the University of Virginia. His research focuses broadly on education policy with an emphasis on teacher policy. Some of his prior work has examined monetary and non-monetary returns to teacher qualifications, strategies rural schools have used to attract and retain teachers, and college attendance and completion rates of rural high school students. Dr. Player publishes in peer-reviewed journals such as *Economics of Education Review*, *Education Finance and Policy*, and the *Journal of Policy Analysis and Management*. He has served on several advisory panels and technical working groups for organizations examining issues related to the teacher labor market including the U.S. Department of Education Institute of Education Sciences, Regional Educational Laboratory— Appalachia, and the J. A. and Kathryn Albertson Family Foundation.

**Angela Rachidi** is a research fellow in poverty studies at AEI, where she studies poverty and the effects of federal safety-net programs on low-income people in America. She is an expert in support programs for low-income families, including the Temporary Assistance for Needy Families and the Supplemental Nutrition Assistance Program. She also studies the effects of tax policy and other benefit programs on low-income American families, particularly on their work and poverty levels. Before joining AEI, Dr. Rachidi spent almost a decade researching benefit programs for low-income populations in New York City.

**Sally Satel**, MD, a practicing psychiatrist and lecturer at the Yale University School of Medicine, examines mental health policy and political trends in medicine. Her publications include, *PC, M.D.: How Political Correctness Is Corrupting Medicine* (Basic Books, 2001), *The Health Disparities Myth* (AEI Press, 2006). *When Altruism Isn't Enough: The Case for Compensating Organ Donors* (AEI Press, 2009), and *One Nation under Therapy* (St. Martin's Press, 2005), coauthored with Christina Hoff Sommers. Her recent book, *Brainwashed: The Seductive Appeal of Mindless Neuroscience* (Basic, 2013) with Scott Lilienfeld, was a 2014 finalist for the Los Angeles Times Book Prize in Science.

**James V. Shuls** is an assistant professor of educational leadership and policy studies at the University of Missouri–St. Louis, where he also serves as the educational leadership program director and assistant department chair for the Educator Preparation, Innovation, and Research department in the College of Education. In this capacity, he teaches principles of school finance to aspiring principals and superintendents. He has authored a primer on Missouri's funding formula, and his work on teacher pensions has been published in the *Journal of Education Finance*. Currently, he is serving as an expert witness in the school finance case *Martinez/Yazzie v. New Mexico*.

**Juliet Squire** is a principal in the Policy and Thought Leadership area at Bellwether Education Partners, where she focuses on school choice, governance, and rural education, among other topics. She most recently worked at the New Jersey Department of Education, where she directed strategies for advancing technology-driven innovation and oversaw the state's Race to the Top program. Previously, she managed school board relationships and new business development for National Heritage Academies, providing support to school leaders and helping launch new charter schools in Louisiana, New York, and Wisconsin. Ms. Squire began her career at AEI, where she studied a wide range of issues in K–12 and higher education policy. She received her bachelor's degree in political science from Yale University.

**Sheneka M. Williams** is an associate professor in the Program of Educational Administration and Policy at the University of Georgia. Her overarching research interest includes students' access to educational opportunity, and her specific research interest includes student assignment policies in urban and rural contexts, school governance, and school-community relations. Dr. Williams is the coeditor of the book *Educational Opportunity in Rural Contexts: The Politics of Place* (Information Age Publishing, 2015). She has also presented aspects of her research at the National Press Club in Washington, DC, and on CNN.